Psalm Prayers

Psalm Prayers

Stephen Cherry

CANTERBURY
PRESS
Norwich

© Stephen Cherry 2020

First published in 2020 by the Canterbury Press Norwich
Editorial office
3rd Floor, Invicta House
108–114 Golden Lane
London EC1Y 0TG, UK

www.canterburypress.co.uk

Canterbury Press is an imprint of Hymns Ancient & Modern Ltd
(a registered charity)

Hymns Ancient & Modern® is a registered trademark of
Hymns Ancient & Modern Ltd
13A Hellesdon Park Road,
Norwich, Norfolk NR6 5DR, UK

British Library Cataloguing in Publication data

A catalogue record for this book is available
from the British Library

978 1 78622 237 4

Printed and bound in Great Britain by
CPI Group (UK) Ltd

Contents

Preface

Towards the beginning of the daily service of Choral Evensong, the psalms of the day are sung in the Prayer Book translation to Anglican Chant. Towards the end of the same service come 'the prayers'. These bring to the mind of the congregation and to the ears of God the concerns that are felt to be appropriate and pressing, and words of thanks and praise that are considered to be apposite.

The psalms and the prayers thus balance each other, presenting human reality and need for God both towards the beginning of the service and near its end. In style, however, they are often extremely different. But while the psalms and prayers play a similar role, they do so very differently.

The psalms are full of unguarded and undefended expressions and sentiments; they marshal concrete language and vivid images to vent feelings in God's direction. They do nothing to take the edge off the sharpness of either life or death; they are bold attempts to put experience and reality in all its actuality – however disorienting, distressing or frankly disgusting – squarely in front of God. By contrast the prayers can sometimes seem polite and guarded and the language in which they are expressed can feel safe and predictable. It's as if the psalms represent what we need to express to God, whereas the prayers reflect what we think God wants to hear.

The psalms express a huge variety of moods and situations and are full of raw human passion and energy. Despite the fact that there is in the Bible a book whose primary purpose is to provide a paradigm of prayer, our actual praying has drifted far from this God-given resource. As Eugene Peterson, pastor and author of *The Message* transliteration of the Bible, has written, 'the Psalms are where Christians have always learned to pray – till our age'.[1]

Not long after I first noticed the gap between the psalms that were sung and the prayers that were often offered at services, I set myself the challenge of writing a new prayer in response to every psalm in the Psalter and was soon offering prayers after the anthem at Evensong that had been inspired by one of the psalms that had been sung that evening.[2] My hope was that some of the ancient authenticity of the psalms would help ground and shape the prayers, and that some of the rawness that characterizes the psalms would remain in the prayers and make them real, despite the obvious fact that our

---

1 Goldingay, Vol. 1, p. 22, quoting Eugene Peterson, *Working the Angles* (Eerdmans, 1987).

2 This is why the version of the psalms in this book are based on the Book of Common Prayer. They are from *The Prayer Book Psalter* by Miles Coverdale (1488–1569), who based his version on the Latin Vulgate and Luther's translation. Coverdale's Psalter did not use italicized words and those used here are to help clarify or emphasize a point.

times are extraordinarily different to those in which the psalms were first used as prayers themselves.

This book is the result. The prayers lie at its heart, but as the collection began to take shape so it became apparent that many potential readers would be helped by a few words that introduced the psalm itself. This is especially the case as everything here is based on the familiar and beautiful, but not always accurate or clear, version found in the Book of Common Prayer. Each prayer is therefore prefaced by a short introduction to the psalm.

Although the psalms vary hugely in length, from the two verses of Psalm 117 to the 176 verses of Psalm 119, these introductions are all of a similar scale. This is because I am not offering a full and objective scholarly commentary on each psalm but an introduction that invites the reader to develop their own relationship with it. The analogy with introducing your guests to each other when hosting a party might help here. You don't spend longer introducing the older people than the younger ones despite the fact that there is often much more that could be said about a 60-year-old person's life story than a teenager's. What you say is hopefully just enough to spark a little friendly interest and curiosity, and then, if you are a good host, you withdraw and find more people to introduce to each other.

After the introduction and the prayer I offer a few words that are intended to spark further refection. These represent another way of responding to the psalm – by identifying and focusing on one of the challenges it presents. The invitation to further reflection is intended to encourage the reader to spend time in the spiritual space that the psalm creates, to meditate further on a particular aspect of it. It is also intended to make the point that our responding to the psalms is not something that comes to an end but is open-ended and limitless. The hope of the 'meditation', even when it concludes with a question, is not to elicit a simple answer but to invite extended reflection on what is going on here spiritually, and what further challenges God might be offering through this psalm at this time.

Books and people

Several books have been especially helpful to me in preparing this work. The commentary by Walter Brueggemann and William H. Bellinger Jr in the *New Cambridge Bible Commentary* series has been very insightful.[3] It is based on the New Revised Standard Version[4] and not only comments on the textual issues, but also offers theological reflections and makes some contemporary connections. Robert Alter's translation with commentary *The Book of Psalms* has the particular strength of not using categories or idioms that are alien to the original, such as 'soul' or 'salvation', and is true to the

---

3 Walter Brueggemann and William H. Bellinger, Jr, 'Psalms', *New Cambridge Bible Commentary* (Cambridge University Press, 2014). Hereafter 'Brueggemann and Bellinger'.
4 Hereafter NRSV.

historical fact that the people who wrote the psalms had no sense of life after death.[5] Alter's reminder of the strangeness of the theological world of the psalmists is apposite.

Another book that has provided inspiration and stimulation is Eugene Peterson's *Psalms*.[6] In his introduction, Peterson makes the point: 'The Psalms in Hebrew are earthy and rough. They are not genteel. They are not the prayers of nice people, couched in cultured language.'[7] His paraphrase is pastorally intentioned, 'I wanted to provide men and women access to the immense range and terrific energies of prayer in the kind of language that is most immediate to them.'[8] Something of the same intention is here, and Peterson's paraphrase has been an inspiration to me, even if I have not quoted from it extensively or followed closely his example in terms of idiom.

It should not be forgotten that the psalms had a huge role of shaping the prayer life of Jesus and his contemporaries. As Trappist monk and writer Thomas Merton explains 'Together with the Our Father, which Jesus Himself gave us, the Psalms are in the most perfect sense the "prayer of Christ".[9] Merton's short book *Praying the Psalms* was another significant influence and resource.

While reflecting on influences on my understanding of the psalms and love of the Prayer Book version, especially when sung to Anglican Chant, I would mention the Directors of Music in the places where I have officiated and offered prayers at Evensong: Sir Stephen Cleobury and Daniel Hyde at King's College, Cambridge, and James Lancelot at Durham Cathedral. The deeply personal care and attention they have given to psalmody in choices of chants, details of pointing and encouragement of their choirs to bring life to the words of the psalms through music, has enriched and grounded the spiritualty of many. This musical ministry not only mediates to human beings a sense of the love and majesty of God, but also nurtures them in a relationship that is at once profoundly intimate and utterly transcendent.

Two friends were kind enough to read an early and incomplete draft of this work: Michael Sadgrove, Dean Emeritus of Durham and Catharine Ogle, Dean of Winchester. I am most grateful for their various comments, questions and suggestions. These have influenced the final shape and style of my attempt to offer an engaging companion to the psalms that encourages the reader to a life-long relationship with them.

Stephen Cherry

---

5 Robert Alter, *The Book of Psalms: A Translation with Commentary* (W.N. Norton & Company, Inc, 2007). Hereafter 'Alter'.

6 Eugene H. Peterson, *The Message: Psalms* (Navpress, 1994). Hereafter 'Peterson'.

7 Peterson, p. 4.

8 Peterson, p. 4.

9 Thomas Merton, *Praying the Psalms* (Martino Press, 2014, p. 11) (emphasis in original). First published in 1956. Hereafter 'Merton'.

Praying with the Psalms

Martin Luther described the Book of Psalms as 'the little Bible', and John Calvin wrote that it provided 'an anatomy of all parts of the soul'. But the Protestant Reformers were not the first Christian enthusiasts for the psalms. In the sixth century, the father of Western monasticism, St Benedict, wrote detailed instructions into his Rule for monks concerning the use of the psalms at their seven daily services, and his communities recited the whole collection every week. So-called Gregorian Chant was later derived to assist and adorn the recitation.

When the Book of Common Prayer was compiled in the sixteenth century the psalms were divided into 60 consecutive portions, one of which was to be read at Morning Prayer and Evening Prayer every day, so that the Book of Psalms was read through every month, so twelve times each year. Anglican Chant was developed as a vehicle for singing the 'Psalms for the Day' by choral foundations and was extensively used by both choirs and congregations in parish churches in the nineteenth and twentieth centuries. Use of Anglican Chant is now much less common in parish churches, but the cathedral and college services at which it is used, notably Evensong, are enjoying a revival in popularity – and Anglican Chant continues to be developed and enriched as a tradition.

Traditional Christian spirituality is therefore based not only on regard and respect for the Book of Psalms as a whole, but also on significant and regular exposure to the 150 different poems in the collection, often mediated by music. Christians are, however, the second readership for the Book of Psalms. The psalms are Hebrew poems written by the Jews across a 500-year period from about 1,000 BCE to 500 BCE. Sadly, there is not a great deal of documentary evidence about how they were used in those days, and so every positive statement made about their origin and early history needs to be seen as a suggestion. The theory that they were used in cultic settings in early Judaism, some of which pre-date the building of the Temple by Solomon, was until recent decades a staple of introductions to the psalms, but more recent writers tend to be more circumspect. As Robert Alter writes, 'Many, but by no means all the psalms were composed for use in the temple cult, though it is worth noting that the elaborate instructions for the conduct of the cult in Leviticus and elsewhere include all sorts of regulations for the preparation and offering of sacrifices but no mandate for songs or liturgical texts.'[10]

It is perhaps odd to contemporary minds that there is a great deal in the Bible about the design and construction of the temple, and a huge amount about when, how and why sacrifices are to be made, but not much at all about how the reading or recitation texts were organized. Alter goes on to warn

10 Alter, p. xvi.

xiii

against the temptation to imagine that we can know more than we do about the original contexts in which the psalms were sung: 'What should be resisted is the inclination of many scholars, beginning in the early twentieth century, to turn as many psalms as possible into the liturgy of conjectured temple rites – to recover what in biblical studies is called the "life-setting" of the psalms.'[11]

Types of psalm

Almost every psalm has a heading or 'superscription'. These short phrases are typically not replicated in collections of psalms intended for liturgical use and, rather unfortunately, those who most regularly engage with the psalms in this way are unlikely to know of their existence. Many superscriptions include the phrase 'A Psalm of David'. Examples include Psalms 3, 6, 23, 32 and 51. However, this should not be taken to mean that David was the *author* of these or any other psalms. The word translated 'of' here (*lĕ*) might equally well be translated in no fewer than six different ways, only one of which denotes authorship.[12]

The truth is that we do not know who wrote the psalms but that it is likely that there were many individuals responsible for the first version of each of the 150 poems *and* that it is probable that there was a significant editorial process over the centuries before the collection became unified and stable. Moreover, as we shall note from time to time, some psalms seem to be compilations of familiar verses that have been aggregated in a particular way to facilitate learning and memory.[13]

The superscriptions have been very helpful to scholars in helping to organize the psalms into different types and groups. Indeed, this sort of analysis has been a significant scholarly project since the pioneering work of Herman Gunkel in the 1960s, and the idea that psalms fall into different genres is now generally accepted. While scholars have disputed, still dispute and will always continue to dispute, quite how many different genres there are and how well each psalm fits into any particular genre, a list of five different genres represents a consensus.[14]

1. Individual and community laments.
2. Hymns of praise.
3. Individual and community thanksgiving psalms.

---

11 Alter, p. xvi.

12 Goldingay lists the six meanings of *lĕ* as: 'to', i.e. 'addressed or offered to'; 'belonging to'; 'for', i.e. as intended for [David's] use or benefit; 'on behalf of', i.e. 'prayed by another for David'; 'about', i.e. 'referring to'; and also 'by', i.e. 'composed by'. Goldingay Vol. 1, p. 27.

13 Given that the psalms were written by many different people, it is not obvious how best to refer to the person who wrote a psalm! I have in the end opted for a variety of words, 'the poet', 'the writer', 'the speaker' and, sometimes, 'the (or a) psalmist'.

14 Brueggemann and Bellinger, p. 5.

4. Royal psalms.
5. Wisdom psalms.

In some places in the Book of Psalms there are short runs of poems that have a similar theme or background and sometimes there are interesting juxtapositions of individual psalms – for instance, compare and contrast Psalms 22, 23 and 24. Such significance and interrelationship cannot be guaranteed.[15] While the Book of Psalms could not be thought of as presenting an argument, the direction of travel is towards God's glory and the human response of praise. That journey goes through every conceivable kind of territory and sometimes there is no apparent reason why one thought follows another. It is worth noting, however, that there are more laments towards the beginning of the collection and more praise songs towards the end. Indeed, the final five psalms all begin with the word 'Hallelujah', usually translated 'Praise the Lord', but that word only appears in Books Four and Five. It is also the very last word of the last psalm in the book.

The Book of Psalms only became a single book after most of the poems in it has been in existence for many years, and that prior to this one book there were, it is agreed by scholars, five shorter collections of unequal length; Book One 1 ends with Psalm 41, Book Two with Psalm 72, Book Three with Psalm 89, Book Four with Psalm 106 and Book Five consists of all the psalms from 107 to the end. Each book concludes with a few verses of praise known as a 'doxology', a word that refers to a short text that declares and celebrates the glory of God, and which is sometimes rather incongruously tagged on to a psalm that didn't seem to be heading in that direction at all. The only exception to this is the fifth and final book, and that is probably because the whole of Psalm 150 is a triumphant shout of praise and, in its entirety comprises the ultimate doxology.

Torah and covenant

This division into five books is understood by many scholars not to be an arbitrary matter but to reflect the division of the Torah, or law of God, into five books. The Book of Psalms has a very close and special relationship to this Hebrew law, and while there are psalms that are absolutely focused on the law, the law of God is not far from the surface of many psalms.

To appreciate this, it is important to realize that in the Hebrew context 'law' does not boil down to the detailed precepts that determine what practices are legal. Certainly, we use the English word 'law' to translate both the Hebrew 'torah' and the Latin word 'lex', but the concepts are very different. This is apparent if you read the five books of the Torah from the beginning and encounter the great narratives of Genesis and Exodus before

---

15 Such links can, however, be found. Michael Sadgrove, *I Will Trust in You* (SPCK, 2009) is subtitled *A Companion to the Evening Psalms*, that is those appointed for Evensong in the Book of Common Prayer, and in it he finds a theme for every grouping of psalms that is clustered together on the same day.

coming to the Ten Commandments or the detailed laws of Leviticus. What these stories make clear is that before any talk of what is right or wrong there is a relationship between God and God's people that is created and sustained by the generous goodness of God. What comes first, then, is what Christians call 'grace' and in Hebrew is 'chesed'. In the Prayer Book version of the psalms this is God's 'loving-kindness' (indeed this expression was created by Coverdale for this purpose). The Hebrew vocabulary here implies that this loving-kindness is 'steadfast'. God's gift is not spontaneous or capricious generosity; it's commitment. 'Law' in Hebrew is intrinsically connected to these notions of 'covenant' and 'loving-kindness', and is a much richer concept than usually comes to mind when we hear the word 'law' in English.

Should this understanding of torah and covenant remind you of the way in which parents relate to their children, then you will be on the right track. However loving, families cannot function without assumptions, memories, shared stories, mutual expectations, boundaries and the like, and we could call these a 'law' that encapsulates the relationships that together go to make up the family and frame their mutual commitments. It is in this sense that torah is the 'law' of God's people, but it is law as in 'a good and wholesome culture that serves the purposes of allowing all to flourish' rather than law as in 'the contents of a book of rules'. And this is where the psalms come in. For the psalmists understand that when human beings fit in with God's law, or abide by the 'ground rules' of God's family, or are faithful to God's covenant as repeatedly offered in the five books of the Torah, then all will be well. When they don't live by the 'law' then everything is out of sync and much goes wrong. The psalms thus promote the Torah, celebrate it and delight in everything that results from life lived within its framework. As Thomas Merton has put it, 'If there is one "experience" to which the Psalms all lead in one way or another, it is precisely this: delight in the law of the Lord, *peace in the will of God*. This is the foundation on which the psalmists built their edifice of praise.'[16]

The psalms have a different tone, however, when experience tells the people that things are not working out well. This is the case, for instance, when people fall short of the demands and expectations of torah. The response then is regret and sorrow – the 'penitence' that finds focused but not exclusive expression in the so-called 'penitential psalms'.[17] Sometimes, however, the feeling is not that the people have let themselves down but that God is not providing the sort of loving protection that torah has led them to expect. The emotion here is disappointment, impatience or even anger with God for not being protective enough and thereby letting the people suffer. So not only do the psalms see the people confessing their sins, but they also see them holding God to account when God does not seem to be keeping faith with the people by honouring their expectations.

---

16 Merton, p. 17. Emphasis original.
17 The designation of six of the psalms as 'penitential' was a sixth century Christian idea. The penitential psalms are 6, 32, 38, 51, 102, 130 and 143.

Again, should this remind you of domestic family life, perhaps at the phase when the children become adolescents, you may not be far from the mark; though it is not typical for adolescents to upbraid their parents for failing to trounce any enemy who has disrupted and disturbed the peace-giving order of the family customs. This is, however, precisely the way in which the ancient Hebrew poems railed against the violence of enemies and the treachery of members of the community who undermined the peaceful order of the community with practices in violation of the Ten Commandments.

The psalms are poems that express the joys and sorrows, the ups and downs, the intimacies and excesses and ultimately the final end of the covenant commitment between God and God's people. To think of the psalms without thinking of torah or covenant, or having a feel for the way life goes when people try seriously to maintain respectful and loving relationships over the long haul and through dramatic crises, is to fail to appreciate much of what is being said, negotiated and hoped for in their verses. But once this is understood it is clear that psalms can in fact offer a model of prayer, because their territory is the whole of life lived in relationship with God.

Ours is a secular culture where an ambient atheism shapes our cultural norms. When we come across injustice our outrage is for the suffering. However, for the psalmists the outrage had a different focus. Not only were people suffering, but even more significantly, God's order had been defiled. This was an insult to God and a violation of torah, but it was also a disappointment because it was God's responsibility to preside over an ordered world. In the introductions, prayers and meditations I have sought to connect the psalms with our own worst and most difficult feelings, but it is important to recognize that the feelings in the psalms are almost always more theological, more overtly and thoroughly connected with God, than are our own today.

God in the psalms

The range and depth of scholarship on the psalms is truly daunting and there is probably no end to the questions that can and will be asked about this extraordinary anthology and the uses to which it has been put over the millennia. This briefest of introductory essays could not be brought to any kind of an end, however, without mentioning two especially important questions: 'who is God in the psalms?' and 'what about the blood-curdling cries for vengeance that are found throughout the collection?'

Two different Hebrew words are understood to refer to God in the psalms. Across most of the Book of Psalms the word used for 'God' is 'YHWH' or, with vowels, 'Yahweh'. The word 'Elohim' also appears in some of the psalms and this is translated 'God', as it is elsewhere in the Bible. This is particularly the case in the Second Book of Psalms: Psalms 41–89. It is Yahweh that is far more common across the Psalter, however. This is the name that was given to Moses at the burning bush when he asked who was speaking; it is the 'I am who I am' (Exodus 3.14). It has not been translated that way, however, but neither has it been translated 'God'. Modern translators often simply don't translate and use the transliterated Hebrew word, with or without vowels, but there is a tradition dating back to the time of Coverdale and the King James Bible of translating 'Yahweh' as 'the Lord' or even 'the LORD'.

Another interesting phrase that is connected with God in the psalms is 'the Lord of hosts'. This is sometimes translated 'the Lord of armies' and is found in situations where force and power are being ascribed to God or invoked, for instance Psalm 46. Another God-question arises in some of the psalms that scholars believe might be very slightly adapted Canaanite songs, the adaptation here consisting of little more than changing the name of God by replacing the Canaanite national deity with 'Yahweh'; see for instance Psalm 29. Related to this are those occasions in the psalms where Yahweh is being promoted and praised not as God, exactly, but as the 'God of all gods', for instance in verse 2 of Psalm 136. This is Yahweh being presented as the best of the many gods, the pick of the bunch of deities. This doesn't sound like a very grown-up way of thinking or talking about God, and such wording is a long way from the sort of theological thought that has developed since the Hebrew tradition came into dialogue with Greek philosophy at around the time of Christ.

So might it not be time to move on from the rather messy understanding of God found in the psalms to something more philosophically precise? Isn't it simply embarrassing to recite poems that God is God, and the only god because God is bigger and better than other gods? This is a very rationalist way of looking at things and while there are merits in this if Christian worship and spirituality is to be constrained by theologically tight expressions of orthodoxy, then our faith, while perfect, will struggle to be a matter of the heart and hands and be in danger of becoming a merely intellectual exercise. Moreover it is likely that some, if not all, of the apparent references to polytheism in the Book of Psalms are actually figures of speech; poetic idioms that point to God's singularity and majesty beyond the powers and forces that otherwise control our lives and imaginations. And herein lies a point about how to engage with spiritual poetry. Yes, the words, and the images they create and feelings they generate in us, do matter, but even more important is that to which they allude, point or otherwise gesture.

No theology is ever adequate, and it is integral to Christianity to seek to be helped in theology, worship and ethics by the words of our spiritual forebears, even when their limits are clearer to us than their merits. This is appropriate not because every word of scripture is 'right' but because every effort to name God is in some way 'wrong'. One response to this is to keep silence before the mystery of God. Sometimes the psalms suggest that this is appropriate, 'Be still and know that I am God' (Psalm 46.10). It is more realistic, however, to see the psalms as a valuable spiritual resource because they take us on journeys of emotional exploration that enrich and renew our spirituality as cognitive, conscious and verbal creatures. That is because they give us words and offer shape to our prayers.

One question that may yet be asked by Christians is 'but is this God of the psalms the God and Father of our Lord Jesus Christ?' Another might be 'is the God referenced in the psalms the Holy Trinity that is worshipped by Christians and believed by them to be bringing all things to their intended fulfilment?' Such questions can't be answered directly but a few points can helpfully be made. One is that the people who wrote these prayers really were addressing God and, unless you embrace polytheism, there is only one God. Another is that Jews and Christians down the years, including Jesus of Nazareth, were steeped in the psalms; they are, as Thomas Merton put it, the 'prayer of Christ'. They are not, perhaps, the last word in enlightened theology or benevolent spirituality or mature faith, but they are tried and tested expressions of human predicament and aspiration before a God who is both known and unknown, who is both with us and yet beyond us.

A spiritual journey

The Book of Psalms is a highly indirect and circumlocutious journey to glory and mystery. We end up in Psalm 150 praising God in God's holiness – although we are not entirely sure what either 'God' means, or 'holiness' is. And while we might choose to ignore its challenges and deny ourselves its insights and delights, the Christian tradition has in its strongest and most influential forms kept faith with the psalms and embraced the journey that they embody and express.

What, then, of the cries for vengeance or the despairing laments? Some of the psalms were clearly written at dark and difficult times, occasions of dispossession, exile, persecution, famine and the like. The five hundred years of their composition and collection had different seasons; but in those days, just as in our own, people didn't turn to heartfelt poetic prayer simply because life was trundling along smoothly and unremarkably. It seems to me, therefore, that it is reasonable, especially if prizing the psalms for their directness, honesty and rawness of expression, not to take a judgmental approach, or to look askance in a spiritually superior way, when we see just how vindictive and violent some of the poems can be.

Rather we should ask, 'what on earth caused these people to want to say this in front of God?' And to go on to ask whether such feelings are ever in our own hearts. If they are, and we can feel with Psalm 12 that the culture we inhabit, the community we live in, is rotten and unreliable, or with Psalm 137 feel the depths of degradation and humiliation known by those who are helpless before merciless captors, then the psalms can be our spiritual friends, giving us permission to explore and interrogate such feelings before God. If not, then the psalms can also be our friends as they can take our imaginations to the extreme conditions in which our spiritual ancestors found that prayer became necessary and vital.

Today we find the expressions of isolation, loneliness and despair in the psalms much more acceptable than we do the vengeful and violent material. This is understandable since no one starts a war because they are catatonically forlorn, but some sense of perspective is necessary too. The psalms offer a safe way of handling dangerous feelings. Take the dangerous feelings out of religion and all you have is space that is so dull and disconnected that people looking for guidance will go elsewhere, for both fun and emotional and spiritual formation.

If we consider the hardest case of all, the final verse of Psalm 137, where a blessing is called upon those who violently murder children, we need not ask 'should we do this?' but ask 'how would we feel if people destroyed our home, transported us to a new environment, deprived us of all we love and enjoy and then mocked and taunted us for not singing and dancing for joy on request?' That's the sort of territory that the psalms invite us to explore. The question is not 'do I approve of some of the more rough-hewn expressions of traumatized people who lived towards the end of the Bronze Age?' but 'can the psalms help us to be honest and heartfelt in our own responses to violations of God's good order and of human dignity?'

Approaching the prayers

The prayers are a mixed bag when it comes to style. Some reflect the register of the Book of Common Prayer and the King James Bible, which was the *lingua franca* of Anglican worship until well into the second half of the twentieth century. This can work well for formal speech, perhaps encouraging a more measured delivery and thereby engendering a sense of spacious reverence. However, the grammar and vocabulary of the sixteenth and seventeenth centuries are not always apt vehicles for thoughts that are more reflective or intimate, and in such prayers I have used a more contemporary style. There is, nonetheless, a degree of formality throughout and the intention is that most of these prayers could be used in public worship.

At the end of the book, is a thematic index of the prayers. This is grouped into three sections. First, those prayers that are most focused on our relationship with God. Second, those that engage with some aspect of life's journey. And third, there are prayers for specific others. There is one entry for each prayer in the index. This should not be taken to mean that the prayers are monothematic; only a few are. Rather it is to provide an indication of the tone of each prayer or the predominant issue it addresses, virtue or blessing it seeks, or reality that it presents.

Of the prayers that are focused on our relationship with God, the largest single category is of those that offer thanks and praise. There is also a good number that in some way ask for, or express, faith and trust in God, and alongside these one might put those that seek a sense of God's guidance or direction. Some prayers here express our desire for God and some our sense of accountability to God.

A similar number of prayers fall into the second category of 'Our journey through life'. It is here that some of our more uncomfortable experiences are brought into prayer under the guidance of the psalmists – there are prayers for use after abuse, harm or trauma, prayers that express our anxiety and fear, and our desperation and despair, as well as prayers in which we express our desire for integrity and holiness and our longing for justice and equity. There are some prayers for which there is only one instance, such as those on ageing, freedom, marriage and that we might learn the lessons of history.

The third category overlaps with the second, but in this case the prayers are focused not on 'us', the generality of people who have a reasonably equitable share in a certain reality or experience, or a desire that can be thought of as not uncommon, but on those who are at the sharp end of one of life's greater challenges. It is in these prayers that we remember the abandoned, the alienated and the lonely, and through them we seek God's help for the betrayed, the demoralized and the dying, as well as the falsely accused and slandered. There are also prayers for those who carry responsibility as civic or religious leaders.

Although we are here praying for 'them' rather than 'us', no suggestion that we should distance ourselves from those for whom we pray is implied. On the contrary, as we pray we seek to make a bridge to the lived reality of all our spiritual siblings and to grow in fellowship and solidarity. Prayer is not a benevolent gesture on the part of those who are close to God on behalf of those who are more distant; it is a humble approach to God made in the company of all who know their need of God. The psalms teach us that it is out of the poverty of our spirit that we pray.

A new song

Thomas Merton once asked why the church is so very keen on the recitation of the psalms. Is it, he wondered, 'because they are ancient, venerable poems?' Does our commitment to them 'come out of conservative refusal to change?' He then ventured the startling but insightful conclusion that 'The Church indeed likes what is old, not because it is old but because it is "young".'[18] His point is that ancient texts such as the psalms matter to us because they are unrefined, unvarnished and unpolished. They represent humanity's relationship with God in a pre-theological, not yet over-thought and super-self-conscious form that is more typical of our efforts to express something of spirituality today. They are of value because they are primitive and raw; like the love letters that people used to write, they come from an early stage in the relationship. When the psalms were written, God and humanity didn't know each other very well. Maybe they still don't. But the relationship still matters and, sometimes at least, needs words.

The psalms are poems of exploration, experimentation and discovery. Psalms 96 and 98 both begin with the phrase 'O sing to the Lord a new song', and others refer to the need for this newness, which we might think of as a fresh spirit or as creativity. The poets who wrote the psalms did not sit down with either the end of their psalm in mind or a formula to hand. This is one reason why the psalms are not at all 'Mills and Boon' and why, even at

---

18 Merton, p. 3.

their most emotional, do not descend into doggerel or sentimentality. This is also why the psalms are often far more robust, abrupt and uncompromising in what they want to say and how they say it than are Christian hymns or contemporary worship songs.

The psalms have emotional and spiritual guts, and if every now and then they are redolent with 'blood and guts' that is because life itself was rough; if there are protests in the psalms it is because life was unfair; if there are laments it is because life was sometimes deeply unhappy. For many people today life is rough, unfair and unhappy. The Book of Psalms is not a book that would be out of place on a battlefield or in a psychiatric prison or a hospice or a refugee camp. Certainly we can hear them sung every day in cathedrals and chapels, but that doesn't mean that they were crafted to entertain us at Evensong. They are recited because our tradition recognizes the truth that pearls of wisdom are not found wrapped up in cellophane and put on sale in gift shops but have to be prized out of oysters that themselves have to be gathered by divers who risk their lungs and their lives with perilous plunges to unfathomable depths.

The psalms remind us that holy truths are dangerous to get and priceless to own. They are presented to us repeatedly so that their youthful directness and ancient beauty might alert us to spiritual honesty and holiness that is neither pious nor otherworldly.

The Book of Psalms may not be quite 'an anatomy of all parts of the soul', as Calvin claimed, but they certainly offer medicine for a wide variety of spiritual ailments and also vintage wine to help us celebrate the joys of life. We should approach the psalms with some respect and perhaps even fear, but chiefly we should approach them with *hope*, not least if we agree with Thomas Merton, that 'Nowhere can we be more certain that we are praying with the Holy Spirit than when we pray the Psalms.'[19] The intention of these introductions, prayers and mediations is to encourage and facilitate such praying, which is of course far more than a matter of words on a page, but also far easier, far more natural and far less guarded than we sometimes dare to believe.

---

19 Merton, p. 11.

Introductions, Prayers and Meditations

Psalm 1: Like a tree

Psalm 1 is an appropriate opening for the whole collection. Its focus is on what a human being needs to flourish, to become 'blessed' or 'happy'. It begins somewhat negatively stating that such a person 'has not walked in the counsel of the ungodly, nor stood in the way of sinners : and hath not sat in the seat of the scornful'. This triple negative is an apt early warning that there are many ways of getting life wrong, which is here characterized as being 'ungodly' or 'wicked'. The way to happiness is to 'delight in the law of the Lord' and to ponder it night and day. This is not law in the modern western legalistic sense, but law as a way of life that is consistent with the nature and the will of God, and will lead to flourishing and fulfilment for all.[20]

The invitation here is to be reflective; to read and inwardly digest the words of Scripture so that they can inform living not as rule book but as deeply ingrained principles. The person who becomes happy, or blessed, is likened to 'a tree planted by the water-side'. Such a tree will be both secure and fruitful because it has roots that go deep into the most helpful source of nourishment. So too with those who reach deep into God's law.

The remainder of the psalm continues this contrast between the blessed and the wicked, who are likened to 'the chaff, which the wind scattereth away from the face of the earth'. The image suggests the light, ephemeral and dissipative nature of the practices, and of those who neither follow God's way not achieve blessedness; the quickly passing nature of the pleasures of those who seek their own way.

The prayer is that we might be given the conditions that we need to flourish.

Bless us, we pray, with the company of people who will enable us to flourish: good friends, a caring community, and wise spiritual guides. Keep us safe from all whose influence would be harmful: the scornful, the cynical, those who seek to manipulate us, and any who hold us in contempt, that we may walk in your way, confident not in ourselves, but in the wisdom and power of your love.

Psalm 1 invites us to ask where we seek spiritual nourishment. Do we dare to delve deeply, or do we foolishly seek sustenance for our more profound needs in superficial comforts?

---

20 See above pp. xv–xvii.

1

Psalm 2: Desire of me

This psalm begins with a strong sense of threat, 'Why do the heathen so furiously rage together : and why do the people imagine a vain thing?' and 'The kings of the earth stand up ... against the Lord, and against his Anointed.' The threat applies to the people and to their king, the anointed one, who represents not only what we call 'law and order' but also the much farther-reaching 'divine order'. The threat is real, but divine power is so invincible as to hold the pretenders in contempt, 'He that dwelleth in heaven shall laugh them to scorn : the Lord shall have them in derision.' Scholars suggest that the psalm is associated with a coronation in Jerusalem, 'Yet have I set my King : upon my holy hill of Sion', and it is categorized as the first of the royal psalms.

The psalm moves to its conclusion in such a way as to leave no doubt as to how those who threaten, or rebel against, the divine order of the Davidic monarchy will be dealt with, 'Thou shalt bruise them with a rod of iron : and break them in pieces like a potter's vessel.' The sense of violence is palpable and, although that is hard to overcome, what we might most want to take from this psalm is the underlying theme that it is trust in God that overcomes fear of enemies.

One verse has a familiar ring to those who know the story of Jesus' baptism, 'Thou art my Son, this day I have begotten thee.' It suggests a loving intimacy that is somewhat lost in the more bellicose sentiments with which the psalm ends.

The prayer is that we might deal well with hostility.

Give us, dear God, the undying conviction that we are your beloved children. Embolden us when conflict and hostility make us fearful, help us to smile when we see the posturing of those who wish us harm. And grant that we, seeking to be wise and peaceful ourselves, may, by our manifest trust in you, inspire peaceable wisdom in others.

Our faith is tested when we find ourselves in a place of turmoil, but this psalm makes the point that it is our faith that will bring us through. Might it always be the case that it is where faith is needed that it is also tested?

Psalm 3: My defender

This is the first in a short series of psalms of lament (Psalms 3–7) and is the personal prayer of someone whose life seems to be going from bad to worse. The writer is oppressed by the hostile stare of many enemies, and also by their mockery. This is not only personal, but extends to the mockery of the faith placed in God and implicit mockery of God, 'Many are saying to me, / 'There is no help for you in God.'[21]

The poet then reports their resolve to call upon God and to adopt a surprising new tactic. The plan is to take a relaxed approach, and avoid the panic reactions so evident as the psalm opened, 'I laid me down and slept, and rose up again : for the Lord sustained me.' This leads on to a commitment not to be afraid whatever happens, though in typical psalmic fashion, the basis of the lack of fear is confidence in the warrior power of God, 'thou smitest all mine enemies upon the cheek-bone; thou hast broken the teeth of the ungodly'. The final verse attributes ultimate and most meaningful power to God, seeing in that the ultimate happiness of God's people.

The prayer is that we might cope well with the threat that comes from others.

> *Protect us, O God, from those who would undermine our faith or wish us harm; rekindle in us the courage that we need to face those who threaten us or bring us trouble; and remind us of the occasions when you have heard our prayer in the past, that we, comforted, consoled and sustained by your grace, may live out our days with faith and in peace.*

The idea that we can be spiritually refreshed by sleep is clearly an ancient one; maybe we should rethink our daily habits from the perspective that sleep is a spiritual issue.

---

21 NRSV.

Psalm 4: Gladness in my heart

This short psalm begins with a request so direct it reads like an instruction to God, 'Hear me when I call.' Before the verse ends, two other imperatives are added: 'have mercy' and 'harken'. This is confident prayer, but it is also needy prayer. It is not the abject grovelling of one for whom a positive answer would be a nice extra in life, but the cry of one who feels their own need deeply. The poet has suffered, as so often in the psalms, at the words of others.

Verse 2 puts three 'vexations' on the table – inflicted shame, vain words and lies (which is the blunt meaning of the archaic, 'seek after leasing'). In verse 3 the tone becomes consoling and then, in the fourth, instructive. The final verses see a change of mood so that the poet comes to express trust in God. This is trust so profound that it leads to a picture of the perfect peace that faith can bring, no matter what people are saying: 'I will lay me down in peace, and take my rest : for it is thou, Lord only, that maketh me dwell in safety.'

The prayer is for freedom from oppression and freedom from self.

Hear our heartfelt prayer, O God of liberty, for freedom: freedom from trouble, freedom from temptation, freedom from loneliness, freedom from vanity, freedom from fatigue, and freedom from need. Let us be so assured of our safety that we may lay down in peace, confident of thy presence, and calm in thy care.

The blunt opening of this psalm invites us to consider whether, and when, we are bold enough to demand God's attention.

Psalm 5: Lead me

There is a strong contrast in Psalm 5 between those who seek to follow the Lord and God's enemies. The psalm is formed of five sections – something not evident from the way in which it is set out in the Prayer Book. The use of language is rhetorical and reflects the style of legal dispute, as is apparent in the opening section where a plea is being made. The second section celebrates God's ethical nature and clarifies that the Lord has disdain, at least, for 'wickedness' and 'evil', 'the foolish' and the vain together with liars, the 'blood-thirsty' and 'the deceitful man'. The third section enumerates those who find favour with God – including the speaker, 'But as for me', and includes a petition for divine leadership and guidance, 'Lead me, O Lord, in thy righteousness, because of mine enemies : make thy way plain before my face.'

In the fourth section the psalmist reverts to the wicked, and piles on the invective with tremendous phrases such as, 'their inward parts are very wickedness' and 'Their throat is an open sepulchre …' God is then instructed to deal with these rebels decisively. The final section is a petition that the faithful might indeed find God's favour and defence.

The prayer is for practical and constructive repentance.

Lead us, Lord, in thy righteousness and make thy way plain before us. Turn our hearts and minds from anything that is mean or cruel or destructive, and from all that is unworthy of us and unpleasing in thy sight. Lift our eyes to the heavens, and let our voices call upon thy love, that we may grow in faith and trust, and come to know true joy and lasting gladness.

Reading this psalm, we might be prompted to wonder about what this notion of 'being favourable to God' might mean in our own day.

Psalm 6: I am weak

This psalm is in the voice of someone who is burdened by their conscience and fearful of where their life is leading. It is the first of the so-called 'penitential psalms', a category invented by the Church in the sixth century. Its drama turns not on the issue of *why* the speaker is in trouble, but on the question of when, if ever, God is going to be of any help. This doesn't quite come across as well as it might in the Prayer Book version, where the trouble is equated with God's punishment and the psalmist's petition is understood as a plea for the end of the punishment 'Lord, how long wilt thou punish me?'

Modern translations make it clear that at this point the speaker is, in fact, lamenting that their trouble has gone on too long, and that there is still no sign of support, mercy or help from God. Robert Alter, for instance, translates, 'Have mercy on me, Lord, for I am wretched / Heal me for my limbs are stricken.'[22] This approach to verse 3 makes a much less abrupt transition to the request for divine deliverance that follows, 'Turn thee, O Lord, and deliver my soul.' The speaker then goes on to lament their lot ever more deeply, and to twist God's arm with the threat of not being able to offer praise should they die in their current state of misery 'who will give thee thanks in the pit?'

We then come across perhaps the most literal expression of inconsolable weeping to be found in the Bible, 'I am weary of my groaning; every night wash I my bed : and water my couch with my tears.' In the final part of the psalm, the speaker rallies, dismisses the troublemakers, and declares that this new-found strength is given by God who has heard both 'the voice of my weeping' and 'my petition'.

The prayer is for those who are weighed down by negativity.

O God, we hold in our hearts those who are burdened with a heavy heart or smothered by depression; those whose souls are troubled and those who feel diminished in the sight of others. We offer to your loving care those who have cried to you by night but found no release; and all who rightly resent the treatment they have received from others. Open their hearts, that they may know the comfort of your love, and restore their sense of calm, dignity and community, that together we may enjoy all the blessings of this life.

Suffering that endures for months or years can have a huge impact on a person and their relationships. What qualities are needed to sustain compassionate relationships over the long haul?

---

22 Alter, p. 15.

Psalm 7: God is provoked

There is a tussle at the heart of this, the final lament psalm in this short series. The speaker is being vigorously pursued but protests their own innocence with equal energy. The protestation continues and the tension is cranked up. The speaker is willing to accept any punishment provided that it can be shown they have done wrong, and God is called upon to act on their behalf. Verse 8 is central to the argument: 'The Lord shall judge the people; give sentence with me, O Lord : according to my righteousness, and according to the innocency that is in me.'

The remaining verses are just as vivid as the early ones and there is yet more tension between the innocent subject, the evil persecutor and the righteousness of God. The speaker is desperate for a hearing and a result, and seems to address their own worry by pointing out that in the end the 'travail', as the Prayer Book has it, or 'mischief' as it is put in several modern translation, rebound on the mischief-maker. The image of evil rebounding is vivid, 'He hath graven and digged up a pit : and is fallen himself into the destruction that he made for other.' This is part of the ongoing and restless struggle to come to terms with persecution, aggravated by false accusation of wrongdoing. The psalm ends somewhat abruptly on a note of thanks to God for being just and dealing justly.

The prayer is rooted in the faith that God will judge rightly.

Hear our prayer, O God, for those who are falsely accused, all who are cruelly slandered and all who suffer the oppression of unjust imprisonment. Free them from their intolerable bondage, and deal justly with those who perpetrate injustice, that we may once again give thee thanks, O God, the God of righteousness.

The request that those who set a trap will fall into it themselves is a common one in the psalms. Is it something we ourselves ever hope or wish for? And is it a sentiment that is compatible with our ideals of justice and kindness?

Psalm 8: How excellent

This, the first poem of praise in the Book of Psalms, begins with abrupt and positive energy. There is no invitation, no 'O come', nor is there any call to the community. There is simply a bold exclamation, 'O Lord our Governor, how excellent is thy Name in all the world.' This is a clear and powerful shout of praise to the creator, which is repeated verbatim as the psalm ends, making this also the first psalm in the book with an 'envelope structure'; a shape in which the beginning finds a strong echo at the end. Within this wrapper we find description, wonder and also a meditative pondering on the human condition. The eyes and ears of the poet are open to the wonder of life, from the intricate tracery of the heavens to the tenacious grip on life of even the youngest of human beings. All this is 'ordained' by God.

But what about us? Where does 'man' fit in? This is poetry, not philosophy or science, and in response to the question the writer focuses first on where humanity fits in the hierarchy of beings, between the earthly and the heavenly creatures and second, where humans are located in terms of 'dominion'. The question that needs most work, it transpires, is not, 'what is man?' but, 'what does "dominion" mean?' The word can be defined as 'authority over', but such authority sits within a larger framework in which, as just mentioned, humanity does not sit at the very top.

What then does it mean to have this 'dominion' over the animals, birds and fish? What responsibility is implied when we are told that all these are 'in subjection under his feet'? That the psalm ends as it begins suggests the answer. Human dominion over 'the works of [God's] hands' really does exist within a framework of responsibility. The point is not so much that we can do what we like but that we are answerable to 'our Governor'.

The prayer is that we might live well as stewards of God's creation.

Most excellent God, your glory so surpasses our knowledge and so transcends our understanding that we wonder about who we are and how we came to be. We study the cosmos and discover that our questions always outnumber our answers. As we give praise for the animals, the birds, the insects and the plants, we lament that even as we delight in them we destroy more than we discover and lose more than we can count. O most excellent God, help us to understand both your glory and our limits, that we might live well in your creation.

In recent years it has become clear that humanity must find a better relationship with the rest of the world than 'exploit and control'. How might the psalmist's belief that God is our 'Governor' begin to repair that relationship?

Psalm 9: Consider the trouble

Psalms 9 and 10 appeared as one psalm in the Septuagint; the Greek translation of the Old Testament made about 200 years before Christ, and the version of the scriptures read by the non-Hebrew-speaking Jews of Jesus' time. They still appear as one psalm in some versions today, which is why some collections of psalms only have 149 psalms. It is also why the numbering of psalms doesn't always line up. The poem known as Psalm 15 in many Bibles is Psalm 14 in the Jerusalem Bible, for instance – and so on.

One good reason for eliding the two is that in the Hebrew an acrostic pattern extends from the beginning of Psalm 9 to the end of Psalm 10. There is further evidence that the two are really one in that, most unusually, there is no superscription for Psalm 10. There is a sense of thanksgiving throughout, though the wording at the beginning of Psalm 9 suggests that the thanksgiving requires resolve and effort, with no fewer than four sentences in two verses beginning 'I will'.

The remembrance of trouble is a strong theme here too, and weaves in and out of the recollection of divine support and praise of God's powerful justice. For instance, although God is warmly praised in verse 11, by verse 13 the psalmist is asking God to 'consider the trouble which I suffer of them that hate me : thou that liftest me up from the gates of death'. The psalm doesn't come to a conclusion but as it moves towards the hiatus that follows verse 20 there is more emphasis on the end of the heathen and the ungodly who fall into their own traps, this being deemed to be the work of divine justice. Perhaps the most central thoughts of this collection of associated ideas are that, 'The wicked shall be turned into hell' and that 'the poor shall not always be forgotten'.

The prayer takes forward the theme of concern for the poor.

Hear with mercy, O Lord, the pitiful prayers of the poor and destitute and give your ear to the humble and meek. Let your loving eye rest on the plight of the oppressed, the bullied, the abused and the excluded; reveal the depths of your care, and rise up in strength to bring true justice to this earth.

The suggestion in the opening verses that effort is required in order to give God thanks is a challenging thought to those of us who have come to see gratitude as an effortless response. Might giving thanks in fact be a form of 'work'?

Psalm 10: Forget not the poor

Although identified as a separate psalm there is good reason to believe that this is in fact an extension of Psalm 9. After the first line the acrostic pattern that began at the start of Psalm 9 is lost for a few verses, which suggests that maybe these lines are later additions, all of which adds to the sense of uncertainty about the origins of this poem and whether or not there is a clear theme running through it. There is a stronger theme of lament here than in the verses of Psalm 9 because the sense of God being distant continues and this means that injustice persists, and that the poor continue to suffer. The ungodly, on the other hand, are still doing very well; they have yet to receive the comeuppance that the psalmist anticipates for them.

It is only in verse 13 that the tide begins to turn. The psalmist has had enough, the God who stands afar off is invited to 'Arise ... forget not the poor.' The verses that follow extend the same petition. God is told that God must have seen what is amiss and is directed to 'take the matter into thy hand'. And if God is in any doubt as to what this taking in hand might involve the next verse spells it out, 'Break thou the power of the ungodly and malicious : take away his ungodliness, and thou shalt find none.' The last phrase here means something like, 'root out all the wickedness in the ungodly until there is none left to find'; perhaps inviting us to picture the careful cleaning of a wound or drilling out of a decayed tooth before it is filled. The final verses return to the theme of praise, perhaps on the basis of hope and trust. Certainly, there is no doubt by the end of this psalm that the God whom the psalmist praises is one who is active in the cause of social justice.

The prayer reflects the somewhat impatient, impassioned and directive tone of the psalm.

Help us to avoid, O Lord, the snares set by the wicked, and by thy great wisdom outwit the cunning of the deceitful. Humble the haughty, subdue the belligerent, undermine the malicious, and stand in the way of those who exploit the vulnerable. And finally, by thy great and abiding mercy, empower the poor, befriend the friendless, house the homeless and let thy kingdom come.

The direct petition that God should break the power of the ungodly and malicious is itself powerful, but remains abstract unless we dare to name the ungodly and malicious. Who or what would be on your list of the 'wicked and evil'?

Psalm 11: My trust

This psalm begins with a confession of trust in God and slowly reveals the need for such a confession. It seems that the psalmist has been advised to run away because of the threat of the ungodly or 'wicked', who are equipped with bows and arrows. But the problem is not just personal; the scale is grand enough to justify worry about what might happen if 'the foundations will be cast down'. Coverdale's version is somewhat misleading in this verse. More recent translations agree that the question is not, 'what hath the righteous done – to trouble the foundations?', but 'what will the righteous do, if, as seems more than likely, the foundations are cast down?' It is at this point that the psalm turns to a consideration of the sense of security that can be found in God who is at home in both earth and heaven and yet engaged with and concerned about the vulnerable.

The rest of the psalm spells out that under the governance of God the game is up for the wicked. There are strong words here. Coverdale wrote that God *abhors* 'him that delighteth in wickedness'; the conviction here is that God actually *hates* 'the lover of havoc' or 'violence'.[23] And this is spelt out in concrete detail of 'fire and brimstone, storm and tempest'. The final verse makes it absolutely plain that God is righteous, that God loves righteousness and that God's face is turned towards the righteous.

The prayer begins with the sense of foundations shaking and ends with the sort of trust with which the psalm begins.

When the foundations of this world are shaking, when we are affronted by corruption, demoralized by lack of leadership and lose trust in our traditions and institutions, draw us, O righteous one, to your constant presence and steadfast love, that we may not despair, but trust ever more profoundly in your goodness and the promise of your justice.

This psalm engages and encourages strong feelings, even challenging us to hate when hatred is called for. When, if ever, might hatred be appropriate?

---

23 Alter has 'havoc', p. 33. The NRSV has 'violence'.

Psalm 12: Pure words

This psalm both begins and ends in sadness. The opening words are a cry for help, but the verses that follow make it plain that for the psalmist the problem here is not a sudden crisis or external threat but some kind of moral sickness that is abroad in the community. As Alter puts it, 'the speaker scans his society in a harsh light of moral castigation'.[24] It cannot be denied that there is some literary pleasure to be found in the verbal expression of such castigation, 'They talk of vanity every one with his neighbour : they do but flatter with their lips, and dissemble with their double heart.' Such is the extent of duplicity and disingenuousness that the speaker doesn't know who to trust or who is worth speaking to. And that is perhaps why they turn to God in this psalm.

The poet here finds faith that God will act, whether this wells up from within or comes from a more confident, external voice. 'I will up, saith the Lord : and help every one from him that swelleth against him, and will set him at rest.' Or, in Peterson's paraphrase, 'I've had enough; I'm on my way / To heal the ache in the heart of the wretched.'[25] The psalm continues by extolling the words of the Lord as 'pure words' clearly a contrast with the corrupted words that issue from 'deceitful lips : and the tongue that speaketh proud things' that are all around. However, the psalm ends where it started, '[and yet] the ungodly walk on every side'. That the issue is not easily or readily resolved is perhaps a testimony to the depth of the problem caused by the corruption of language.

The prayer is for the worthy use of the power of language.

O God, bless all people of influence with the gift of truthful speech and clear writing; and curb the tongues of all who are tempted to use cruel, contemptuous or hateful words. Give to us all the desire to speak kindly and to use the power of language to engender trust in our community and justice in our society.

We live in times when suspicions run high, and it is extremely difficult to live well if you feel you cannot trust the customs or institutions of your own society. What forms of spiritual resistance might the psalms suggest when trust is low?

---

24 Alter, p. 35.
25 Peterson, p. 18.

Psalm 13: How long?

The opening verses of this short psalm are the cry of one who, afflicted by grief or illness, feels absolutely forgotten. This poor soul is completely out of patience. The four-fold repetition of 'how long?' in verses 1–2 shows us someone who has come to the limit of their ability to cope. The verses say in no uncertain terms, 'I have had enough. I am done with this.' The speaker wants attention; it is time for acknowledgement and response. Action is called for in the curious phrase 'lighten my eyes', which means 'brighten them' or 'light them up'. God is even given a reason to attend and act – that opponents and enemies might be taking pleasure in the misfortune. Verse 5 begins with the word 'but', and thereupon the tone of the psalm changes completely.

'But ...'

We might reasonably wonder whether in real time verse 5 can follow on immediately from verse 4. Patrick Woodhouse suggests that there is a 'great silence' between the verses. 'Somehow, the questioning, the articulation of the despair, the very direct outburst into the void where God does not seem to be ... has done its work. ... There appears to have been a visitation. Into the anguished emptiness of this person's soul, grace has entered, like balm on a raw wound.'[26] Certainly there is a change in feeling and outlook. Lament has led to plea and without any sense of how the plea is answered we arrive at a statement of trust and joy and then a burst of thanks and praise. This is not what one might expect from someone who is on the edge of despair, but rather from a person who has just received the most wonderful news : 'I will sing of the Lord, because he hath dealt so lovingly with me : yea, I will praise the Name of the Lord most Highest.' The words of the psalm are powerful and moving, but the turning point is not narrated at all. It happens in the space where there are no words.

The prayer mirrors the shape of the psalm and is intended for occasions when spirits are very low.

> *Look upon us, O Lord God, in our isolation and estrangement. Do not abandon us to grief or let us sink into deep, dark sadness. Visit us in our lonely distress. (A silence may be kept.) Brighten our eyes, O God, with the dew of thy grace, that our souls may once again trust in thy loving-kindness and our hearts sing out with joyful praise.*

Psalm 13 challenges us both to name our sadness and to keep silence in the hope that silence itself might make a space in which God can act for us. Might it be that our greatest gift might sometimes not be our words but our hopeful silence?

---

26 Patrick Woodhouse, *Life in the Psalms: Contemporary Meaning in Ancient Texts* (Bloomsbury, 2015), p. 234. Hereafter, 'Woodhouse'.

Psalm 14: An open sepulchre[27]

Although this rather unusual psalm reads like a description, it is actually crafted as a bit of practical wisdom for the young to take to heart. The method is to expose the way of folly so that it might be avoided. The logic of such reverse pedagogy is that if someone is to grow up wise they must know something of the way in which fools think and act. But there is an intellectual trap in verse 1. The 'fool' here does not doubt the existence of God *per se*. Rather, they doubt whether God will care or respond to any of their acts and they therefore live with a sense of impunity. In short, the psalm is not about atheism, but about accountability. Verse 3 is perhaps the subtlest and most touching. 'The Lord looked down from heaven upon the children of men : to see if there were any that would understand, and seek after God.' The answer comes in the negative, and is followed by several interpolated verses,[28] which vividly describe those who have 'gone out of the way' and have 'altogether become abominable'. Not only are such people unattractive and foul-mouthed, but they are also rapacious, 'eating up my people as it were bread'. But the faith here is strong. God will sort it all out in the end 'for God is in the generation of the righteous' and all ends well 'then shall Jacob rejoice, and Israel shall be glad'.

The message is clear and familiar 'it is wise to live with a sense of accountability to God'. In this psalm the poor are vindicated, and those who live accountably are rewarded. Verse 10 is a significant rebuke for the ungodly, 'As for you, ye have made a mock at the counsel of the poor : because he putteth his trust in the Lord.'[29] It is this thought that gives this version of familiar teaching its distinctive flavour.

The prayer seeks to apply the wisdom of living with a sense of accountability to God.

> *O God, this world is full of pride and hypocrisy: arrogance abounds, folly reigns, and true wisdom is mocked. Help us to understand our accountability to your judgement and to follow the path of grace and truth until we come to the joy of knowing your will, embracing your freedom and accepting your salvation.*

This psalm challenges us to appreciate that the greater our faith in God the more we will accept that we are accountable to God. What might this mean in terms of personal freedom and social justice?

---

27 Psalm 14 is also found in a modified form as Psalm 53, which ensured that this teaching is also included in the Second Book of the Psalms.

28 The interpolated material is only found in the Book of Common Prayer version and comes from elsewhere in the Psalter. These verses are quoted alongside verses that do belong in Psalm 14, in Romans 3, which perhaps persuaded Coverdale, or those who compiled the sources from which he was working, to interpolate them here.

29 Verse 10 is not replicated in Psalm 53, which changes the emphasis.

Psalm 15: An uncorrupt life

While Psalm 14 was concerned with the character and end of the foolish and ignorant who ignore God, Psalm 15 is interested in the qualities of those who might come into God's presence – the righteous. Some argue that its origins were in a ritual that would have taken place at the entrance to the Temple, though Alter dismisses the suggestion that this might be 'a set of questions posed by priests or Levites to the arriving pilgrims'.[30]

Nonetheless the psalm is a list, and a straightforward one. There is no use of metaphor, no imagery; it is not theologized, and there is no suggestion that as we are all ultimately unworthy, we can only be admitted by the grace of God. No, the ethics are plain enough. Behave thus and you will be allowed to visit God's tabernacle and rest on God's holy hill. The question 'what if I don't or can't?', isn't asked and isn't answered. The message is simple, do the right thing and speak the truth.

The prayer is for faith and integrity.

> *Receive our prayer, O God, and grant that we may enter into thy presence, and, so that we may be prepared to receive thy welcome, enable us to act justly and to speak straightforwardly, to retain a kindly and humble disposition, and to keep our promises, neither disappointing our friends nor exploiting the vulnerable.*

This psalm invites us to think of the people whom we look up to as our moral exemplars. How far do the people you admire meet the criteria of this psalm?

---

30 Alter, p. 43.

Psalm 16: A goodly heritage

This psalm is both an expression of confidence in God and a prayer for faith. Some of the language is memorably beautiful : 'The lot is fallen unto me in a fair ground : yea, I have a goodly heritage', 'my flesh also shall rest in hope'. The psalm opens with the word 'Preserve', which begins its most important petition. And yet today the verb doesn't have a very positive or helpful resonance. Nor do various others that appear in more recent translations, for instance, 'protect' or 'guard'.[31]

The psalm is fundamentally a confession of faith, and yet offers clues to those seeking to find genuinely sustainable ways of living. These include the point that we should value God more than material goods, admire the genuinely virtuous, avoid false gods and being drawn into unhealthy practices, give thanks for what is good, be grateful for divine guidance or rebuke, and always focus on God. All this makes practical sense because God's will is benevolent. The final verse serves as an apt summation. 'Thou shalt show me the path of life; in thy presence is the fullness of joy : and at thy right hand there is pleasure for evermore.'

The prayer is that we might be sustained in faith.

Sustain us, O God, for we have put all our trust in thee and our greatest delight is to be in the company of the faithful. Bless us with the gifts of patient hope and of loyalty to thy love, that we might find fulfilment in the joy of being close to thee for ever.

The question of the spirituality of 'sustainability' is an urgent and contemporary one. To what extent do you find wisdom to guide sustainable living in this or any other psalm?

---

31 'Protect' is NRSV, 'Guard' is Alter, p. 45.

Psalm 17: The apple of an eye

This psalm is the prayer of a person who has been falsely accused and who seeks protection from their enemies. It begins with the speaker both professing their faith and protesting their own innocence. This is not self-righteousness, exactly, but a claim to have been faithful and in particular to have avoided violence, 'the ways of the destroyer'. It is in the second section of the psalm that its particularly strong character is revealed. God is petitioned to show 'marvellous loving-kindness'. This verse alludes to the memory of the exodus of the Hebrew slaves from Egypt; the speaker is looking for significant and transformative action from God.

The intimacy with which the psalm began is soon rekindled, 'Keep me as the apple of an eye : hide me under the shadow of thy wings.' The 'apple of an eye' is the image of yourself that you can see when looking into the eyes of another. The 'wings' are those of the cherubim over the Ark of the Covenant. These twin images invite the close protection of God. The verses that follow explain why it is needed by describing the sources of threat in equally vivid ways. The 'fat' in which they are 'inclosed' is around them. Goldingay comments: 'Closing the midriff implies being unwilling to rethink their attitudes and their lives.'[32] The same verse notes that 'their mouth speaketh proud things'. 'Proud things' refers to arrogant and unaccountable speech. As one translation puts it, 'They close their heart, / they mouth contempt'.[33] The enemies also lie in ambush seeking to cast their victim (not their eyes) to the ground and are likened to lions. The petition is then intensified. God is roused so that the enemy may be 'disappointed' and 'cast down'.[34]

The final two verses return to the tone with which the psalm began, offering a prayer that the protection of God will be good not only for now but also for generations to come. The final verse offers a profound image of personal beatitude.

The prayer is for protection.

Hear us, O God, as we pray for protection from those who hold your ways and your servants in contempt. Keep us close and shield us under your wings. Witness our striving to be faithful in the face of adversity, indifference and scorn, that strengthened by your presence we might reflect your glory, and, in the fullness of time, see you face to face.

Psalm 17 encourages us to be honest about how we feel when we are the subject of unkind words or false allegations. Might it also help us find the right course of action after such an unwelcome, though sadly not unlikely, life-challenge?

---

32 Goldingay, Vol. 1, p. 242.
33 Caroll Stuhlmueller OP, *The Book of Psalms* (Liturgy Training Productions, 1995). Hereafter, Stuhlmueller. NB The pages are not numbered in this Psalter.
34 Alter translates this as 'Rise, Lord, head him off, bring him down', p. 50.

Psalm 18: My strong helper

This epic and energetic poem is the second of the royal psalms and understood by many to be a poem-prayer of David himself. It is also found in 2 Samuel 22. After a powerful introductory section in which David's love of God is proclaimed and God's ready protection is celebrated the psalm turns to narrative. David is in serious trouble and calls upon God – there follows a section that offers all the thunder and drama of the appearance of God to Moses on Mount Sinai, in which God becomes active. After this preamble God reaches down for the actual act of rescue and deliverance in verses 16–20.

The verses that follow clarify that David was worthy of this rescue as he was faithful to God. The next section describes and praises God's righteous nature. This leads on to a rich and unadulterated song of triumph and victory before the whole great psalm concludes with a verse in praise of God who is proclaimed faithful to David and David's line for ever, 'Great prosperity giveth he unto his King : and sheweth loving-kindness unto David his Anointed, and unto his seed for evermore.'

The prayer celebrates the practical, saving love of God.

Beloved Lord, you are my rock and my defence. When I was in darkness, you brought me light. When I was weak, you renewed my strength. When I was brought low, you gave me the feet of a deer and I scaled new heights. When I was threatened you emboldened me to resist. And so I offer my heartfelt thanks, I sing your praise and renew my commitment to live by faith and trust, now and always.

This song of praise after rescue invites us to reflect on our own experience of being brought to safety when in danger and, whether our experiences were dramatic or mundane, how we feel about our rescuers.

Psalm 19: The glory of God

There are two schools of thought about this psalm. The more ancient view is that it is one psalm and that it invites us to integrate our mediations on the natural world with those on God and God's law or torah. Then there is the more modern opinion that this is, in fact, two different poems. The first is about creation, while the one that follows concerns the torah.

There are, however, real advantages in viewing this as one psalm. Not only is it likely that many biblical texts are formed by a process of multiple edits drawing together material from different sources, but it may also be that such an editorial process is as inspired as the original writing of one word after another. Given the way in which Judeo-Christian history has often alienated the natural world from higher purposes there is especially good reason to let a text that integrates them speak to us; to let ourselves hear the power of the testimony that although there is neither speech nor language, 'The heavens declare the glory of God : and the firmament sheweth his handy-work.'

As the psalm progresses, the sun comes in for especially close attention and this sets the scene for the praise of the power and wisdom of torah. Indeed, when taken as a whole, the arc of this psalm reaches from the highest of heavens to the depths of personal integrity. Towards the end there are touching insights into some of the more mysterious ways of the heart: the inability to know how often we sin and the difficulty of avoiding sins of presumption. Interesting here is that it is not the sin or presumption *per se* that is identified as problematic but the risk that 'they get the dominion over me' and lead on to 'the great offence'. These lead on to the famous final words, which pray that 'the words of my mouth, and the meditation of my heart : be always acceptable in thy sight'.

The prayer reverses the shape of the psalm.

O God, our rock and redeemer, direct our thoughts that we may meditate wisely and speak with due care. Inspire us to see thy glory in all thy works that we may come to understand more fully the truths that words cannot tell.

The idea that sins of presumption can lead on to 'the great offence' is a challenging one to modern people. Maybe we have forgotten that a faithful response to God is one that embraces healthy humility and avoids toxic pride.

Psalm 20: Thy heart's desire

This, the third royal psalm, invokes the help of God at a time of national crisis, which is understood as an especial crisis for the monarch. It has a neat envelope structure beginning with a plea that God will 'hear' and ending with the petition that God will 'Save ... and hear us.' Interestingly, the psalm refers to the 'the Name' of God on three occasions, as if the name itself had agency, or was an intermediary with the absolute sovereignty of God. The point here is not that names bestow power on the person who does the naming or uses the name of another person. Rather the appeal to God's name is the appeal to God's *character*. The poet knows that 'the Lord helpeth his Anointed'. This is what God does because God is good. Certainly, 'Some put their trust in chariots, and some in horses' but this is to no avail because 'They are brought down, and fallen.'

The message is that it is not enough just to have faith, or to place trust carelessly. For faith to be of value it needs to be faith in what is faith-worthy, just as worthwhile trust must be in that which is trustworthy. We might also say that it is wise only to love that which is worthy of love. And the name for ultimate trustworthiness, faith-worthiness and love-worthiness is the name of God.

The prayer is for mature faith.

Hear our prayer that we offer to thy name, good Lord, that we may grow in faith, in trust and in love. Help us to put our faith in thee and empower us to trust thee; and so shape our hearts that we may always reach out to thee in love, that by thy grace and guidance we may attain the full stature of thy beloved.

The clear imperative here is to trust in God come what may. This might make us ponder the difference between a life based on trust and a life based on suspicion.

Psalm 21: Everlasting felicity

This is the fourth royal psalm. It has a tidy structure, beginning and ending with a verse of praise. In verse 1 it is the praise of the king, 'The King shall rejoice in thy strength, O Lord.' In the final verse it is the praise of the whole community, 'So will we sing, and praise thy power.'

Between these verses the psalm is cleanly divided into two sections. The first, verses 2–7, is the recollection of the bestowal of blessings and of acts of deliverance. The second, verses 8–12, looks forwards to the future as a time when God will also be victorious over all enemies. The pattern of remembrance and forward-looking-ness, wrapped in an envelope of praise, honours well the claims of the past, the present and the future.

The prayer is that we might balance appreciation of the past with prudent orientation to future danger.

Grant, O Lord God, that all who trust in you may appreciate their blessings, value their life, and know joy and gladness in their hearts. Help us to resist those who pose a physical threat to us, and do not let us be intimidated by those who hold us in contempt. Shield us from dangers yet to unfold and draw us ever closer to your love, that we may forever sing your praise.

Sometimes we feel nostalgically attracted to the past and on other occasions we are naively optimistic about the future. This psalm challenges us to consider whether we favour the past, the present or the future.

Psalm 22: Look upon me

The opening words of this psalm, 'My God, my God … why hast thou forsaken me', would be arresting even if they were not attributed to the dying Jesus in the gospels. And yet these words are not intended to stop us in our tracks, but to draw us forward. First, in the first 21 verses, to the horrific experience of abandonment and torture; and in the remainder of the psalm to some kind of new life that is celebrated towards the end of this psalm.

What is most interesting about the psalm, however, is the intermingling of the experience of suffering and faith. It is '*my* God' who has done the forsaking, suggesting that some kind of intimate relationship remains. And in the verses that follow, it is not always clear whether the past is being remembered with deep regret, since all that was good about it seems to have come to nothing, or whether it is in fact a reservoir of memories that actually sustain the suffering psalmist.[35] There is no such ambiguity in the verses which resonate more directly with the crucifixion of Jesus, 'They pierced my hands and my feet … and cast lots for my vesture.' Verse 21 is the turning point, despite the terrible suffering that has been foregrounded and the imminent threat of death.

Nonetheless God somehow hears this desperate prayer and in the remainder of the psalm the focus changes from personal suffering to the praise of God who 'hath not despised, nor abhorred, the low estate of the poor'. In fact, the vision of humanity praising God that emerges is wide and expansive and even incorporates the departed and those of generations yet to come.

The prayer expresses tentative hope after devastating degradation.

Hear our prayer, O God, for all who, this day, feel abandoned as they face mockery, humiliation, abuse or torture. Give them the courage to face their afflictions, and inspire in them a sense of fellowship with others who suffer and the hope that their lonely tribulation will soon end.[36]

This psalm clearly speaks to people powerfully, perhaps because we know at some deep level that we need to bring our most desperate thoughts, feelings and experiences into our prayers with tired but not yet defeated longing.

---

35 This is a suggestion made by Woodhouse, p. 254.
36 This is a version of the same prayer that might be used in private.
> *My God, I whisper to you in the darkness of my despair, hoping that no one else will hear. As a child, I grew accustomed to your warmth and your love, as I prayed in the comfort of my bed and enjoyed the blessings of food, shelter and parental love. But now all that is gone. I am ruthlessly exposed, and powerless in the face of the assaults that rain upon me by day and by night. Yet even this whisper is a prayer; even this whisper is a token of trust. So I will let it swell to a cry in which I no longer lament your absence, but praise the possibility of your presence and offer this, the only prayer that remains in my melted heart: that if I die, I may rise with you.*

Psalm 23: The waters of comfort

Almost certainly the most famous, most often recited and best-loved psalm, 'The Lord is my Shepherd' is certainly one 'affecting simplicity'.[37] But it is perhaps a richer feast for the soul than we sometimes realize, our familiarity dulling our perception. It certainly begins with an image of God as the diligent and competent carer and guardian who provides for all our needs, even those that we don't know that we have: 'therefore can I lack nothing'. The shepherd image must have had a powerful impact on people who lived in agrarian and pastoral communities, but the whole collage of images of Psalm 23 still touches us today, not least the irresistibly refreshing thought of 'the waters of comfort' – waters that are 'quiet' or 'still'.

There is a subtle transition in verse 3, which sees revival of the soul, new life, and a reorientation to righteousness or justice, and perhaps even a hint of forgiveness. Immediately, however, we hit the shadow side, a dry gorge so deep that the sunlight never reaches the bottom, 'the valley of the shadow of death'. But even in such literal or metaphorical darkness there is no reason for fear, and the tone is even more intimate; God is not described but addressed, 'thou art with me'. Indeed, the shepherd now becomes host to a good meal, an overflowing cup[38] and a head anointed with oil – and all this in full glare of the enemies.

The final verse comes to the heart of the matter. God's 'loving-kindness and mercy', which haven't so much 'followed' as 'pursued' me, 'all the days of my life'.[39] Finally, even though the message so far is that God has found us in the great outdoors, the desire is to 'dwell in the house of the Lord for ever'.

The prayer is that God will be present to us throughout our life's journey.

O Shepherd of all, give us, we pray, a profound sense of your loving-kindness, lead us in the paths of righteousness, comfort us when we wander and, in your good time, guide us through the valley of the shadow of death to the green pastures and the peaceful waters of your eternal, plenteous and peaceful kingdom.

Perhaps the main challenge of this psalm is to understand its astonishing popularity. What have we yet to learn about human yearning from Psalm 23?

---

37 Alter, p. 78.
38 The Book of Common Prayer has it that the psalmist's cup is full, but more recent translators agree that it overflows.
39 'Pursued' is the verb used by Alter, p. 80.

Psalm 24: The King of glory

This is a psalm in three parts. It begins with two verses that proclaim the power of Israel's God and rehearse the claim that it is the God called 'Yahweh' who is, in fact, the only one powerful enough to subdue the forces of chaos. This theme is also strong in the final section which speaks of 'the Lord strong and mighty, even the Lord mighty in battle' and incorporates the phrase 'Lord of hosts' which is often translated 'Lord of armies', reinforcing the sense that it is the power of God that is in focus here.

The middle section of the psalm, verses 3–6, is about something else. It concerns the qualities of those who may 'ascend into the hill of the Lord'. This is reminiscent of Psalm 15 and the question asked is fundamentally the same, 'who is ethically fit to enter into God's city, Jerusalem?' The answer comes in terms of purity and simplicity; in short it is individuals of integrity who together make up a company (or 'generation') of integrity who may 'rise up in his holy place'. What unites the second and third section of the psalm is the sense of ascent and arrival. It is curious that the arrival of the Ark of the Covenant is celebrated last in this psalm, but perhaps it hints that even before that auspicious occasion, recorded in 2 Samuel 6, there was something about the hill of the Lord that demanded integrity of those who might approach it.

Taken as a whole, the psalm is about a holy place and holy people. The place derives its holiness from the power of the great God; the people derive their holiness from their simplicity and integrity.

The prayer is that we may approach the holiness of God with integrity.

Eternal God, we see thy face in the beauty and order of creation. Give us, we pray, clean hands and pure hearts, integrity of speech and simplicity of purpose, that as we approach thy holy place we may be granted a vision of thy powerful and radiant glory.

This psalm encourages us to put a high value on integrity, but pure integrity may not only be rare but impossible to achieve. The dauntingly high standards of this psalm might make us wonder whether there can be a 'good-enough' form of integrity.

Psalm 25: Show me thy ways

Psalm 25 is a series of petitions to God, mingled with some strongly expressed imperatives, and interspersed with moments of reflection. It is written as an imperfect acrostic, which explains the absence of 'flow' from one verse to the next in translation. There is nothing unique about this psalm. All the ideas expressed here are found elsewhere in the Psalter, most in expanded form.

The psalm begins and ends with short statements of need and petition, in between, Brueggemann and Bellinger identify five themes.[40] The speaker faces a dire emergency but has confidence enough to wait on God; hope is in the reliability of God's steadfast love ('loving-kindness' in Coverdale's translation); the speaker emphasizes their own integrity and reliance on God. There is, in parallel, open confession of sin and inadequacy; both 'fidelity and failure' or integrity and sinfulness are put forward as reasons for needing and seeking God's involvement and action. Where Coverdale uses the word 'perfectness', the King James Bible and NRSV both use the word 'integrity'. It is apt: there is a strong desire for integrity before God here.

The prayer is for help in a time of crisis.

> *Lead us, Lord, from our current crisis to a place of safety, and, as we recall our afflictions and troubles, help us not to forget our personal record of wrong, or fail to recollect the ground of our hope. Keep our eyes fixed on the reliability of your love, that the troubles of our hearts may be eased, for unto you, O Lord, do we lift up our souls.*

Reflecting on this psalm we might go back to its point of departure, a dire emergency, and ask ourselves two questions. First, how did I respond last time I faced real and urgent difficulty? And second, how would I hope to respond next time?

---

40 Brueggemann and Bellinger, pp. 1312.

Psalm 26: Examine me

The protestations of personal innocence with which Psalm 26 begins mean that is not the most instantly attractive of psalms. 'Be thou my judge, O Lord, for I have walked innocently.' The writer goes on to advertise their own faithfulness and their habit of avoiding bad company. Verses 6 and 11 both speak directly of the innocence of the speaker's practices, though a close reading suggests that these are not so much reports of actions as of intentions or promises. Nonetheless there is at least a hint of priggishness in the description of those of whom the psalmist disapproves when followed by, 'But as for me, I will walk innocently.' The claim to love God's dwelling also comes across as somewhat holier than thou, 'Lord, I have loved the habitation of thy house : and the place where thine honour dwelleth.'

However, if we begin to think of these verses as written by someone falsely accused and judged and now going to appeal in a higher court, rather more sympathy may be kindled. Now the language is not so much boastful as desperate. And, while we might yet feel uncomfortable at someone pleading their own cause with such thoroughgoing self-praise, the speaker in the psalm does indicate a positive and moral approach to life; especially if the plea in the first and penultimate verses is that the speaker be regarded not as entirely 'innocent', as it is often put in older translations, but that they have 'integrity' – a theme we found in the previous psalm. Read like this, the psalm is an extended invitation to God to 'look into my heart and judge what is really there, and do not be persuaded by what others say about me'.

The prayer is a plea for divine assistance to live with integrity.

Help us to trust in your justice, O God, as we seek to live our lives with integrity. Keep the vision of your loving-kindness always before our eyes, and encourage in us a love of your people and your house, that our character may be formed by your saints and shaped by holy tradition. Keep us faithful in prayer and worship, and guide us away from those whose influence on us might be destructive, and any who would deceive us with false kindness. O God, help us to live our lives with integrity, to offer praise in the company of the righteous, and to seek out the place where your glory abides.[41]

Coming across in the wrong way to other people is something that happens to us all, and it is perhaps most likely when we feel defensive. Has your defensiveness ever been interpreted as boastfulness or hostility?

---

41 The final sentence could stand as a prayer on its own.

Psalm 27: Seek my face

Psalm 27 is one in which the parallelism of Hebrew poetry comes through especially strongly, and from verse 1 gives a sense of depth, inviting a slowing of pace, a moment of respite from the rush of life. This is a psalm that encourages a contemplative and confident approach to life. 'The Lord is my light and my salvation; whom then shall I fear : the Lord is the strength of my life; of whom then shall I be afraid?'

The psalmist expresses considerable insecurity in these verses; but the insecurity is more than met by faith and trust in God. This is most profoundly and poignantly seen in a verse that suggests the root of the anxious insecurity that emerges through the psalm, at the same time as finding a deeper security beyond it: 'When my father and my mother forsake me : the Lord taketh me up.' Perhaps the writer of this psalm is a young person struggling with the insecurities inflicted by unreliable parenting or abandonment. In verse 5 the words translated 'tabernacle' and 'dwelling' are 'drawn from the lexicon of nomadic habitation'.[42] Their flimsiness stands in vivid and jarring contrast to the third noun used in the same verse, the 'rock of stone' on which the psalmist understands that God will ultimately 'set him up'.

There is a rich vein of longing expressed in the psalm. This is focused on the desire to abide in God's place, but it extends to the hope of seeing God's face, something denied even to Moses. So maybe we are seeing some of the spiritual passion as well as the emotional insecurity of a young adult here. And for all the apparent desire for peace with God, there is liveliness in the penultimate verse, which hopes to see 'the goodness of the Lord in the land of the living'. In the final verse there is a strong emphasis on patiently waiting and trusting, 'Wait for the Lord; / be strong, and let your heart take courage; wait for the Lord!'[43]

The prayer is that we might live with contemplative awareness and calm.

Teach us, O God, the wisdom of waiting. Renew in us the desire to spend our time in your presence, meditating on your love and appreciating your beauty. Cleanse us of the toxins of anxiety and fear, and give us the patience, trust and hope that we need to live faithfully and well.

Emotional insecurity can be deeply problematic, but might it be that *awareness* of emotional insecurity is actually vital for genuine maturity?

---

42 Alter, p. 92, who prefers the words 'shelter' and tent'.

43 The NRSV translation is quoted here, where the numbering is different and this is verse 14. In the BCP it is 16 and reads, 'O tarry thou the Lord's leisure : be strong, and he shall comfort thine heart; and put thou thy trust in the Lord.'

Psalm 28: I cry unto thee

Psalm 28 has the classic structure of a psalm of lament. It begins by vividly articulating need and desperation, 'Unto thee will I cry, O Lord my strength' but after a few verses there is a wonderful change of mood and light appears, 'Praised be the Lord : for he hath heard the voice of my humble petitions.'[44] Indeed it brightens very dramatically in verse 8, 'The Lord is my strength and my shield; my heart hath trusted in him, and I am helped : therefore my heart danceth for joy, and in my song will I praise him.' The following verse refers to 'the Anointed', and whether this is a reference to the king or God's people as a whole, all are definitely included in the final verse, where it is 'the people' whom God is asked to save.

The dramatically positive ending is all the more vividly impressive when we appreciate the depth of desperation with which the psalm began; it was a last gasp. The speaker fears that if not heard, 'I [will] become like them that go down into the pit.' Or, to put it more succinctly, 'Without you I must die.'[45] There is, then, a 'mood swing' as Brueggemann and Bellinger put it, at verse 6.[46]

Scholars have speculated as to how this might have originated. Were the final verses added later? Was there some kind of liturgical hiatus before verse 7 when the psalm was recited, and the brighter words introduced? Such mood-swings, whether from lament to thanksgiving or from despair to hope, are a vivid feature in several psalms.

The prayer is intended for personal use when despair descends.

Hear this prayer of mine, O my God, which comes from deep in my inner pit of despair. Hear me, O my God, hear me before it is too late! Speak to me words of comfort! Bring to me healing! Shield me from further danger and draw me from this dreadful place! Be a source of new strength for me, I pray, that my heart may once again dance for joy and my prayer be full of praise.

Several psalms challenge us to reflect on what might bring an upturn when we are at our lowest ebb. Their message is simply this, 'Put your most negative stuff in front of God in unvarnished prayer, and see what happens.' But do we dare?

---

44 Or in Alter's translation, 'Blessed is the LORD / for he has heard the sound of my pleading.' Alter, p. 96.
45 Stuhlmueller.
46 Brueggemann and Bellinger, p. 145.

Psalm 29: The voice of the Lord

This psalm is so different, distinctive and vivid in its style and imagery that many have argued that it was originally a hymn of the Canaanite people in praise of Baal, the storm god who rides upon the clouds. The idea is that the early Hebrew people heard and appreciated such a hymn and simply changed the word 'Baal' to 'Yahweh'. However, this theory is no longer in scholarly vogue. Indeed, Brueggemann and Bellinger suggest quite the opposite, that there could be 'an anti-Baal polemic' at work here.[47]

It begins with a call to worship and the middle part of the psalm is a celebration of the goodness and power of the voice of God. The final two verses are a praise-filled description of God's majesty and might that introduces petitions that God might give the people 'strength' and bless them with 'peace'. The bulk of the psalm, then, celebrates the powerful ways in which God is made known, and uses the imagery of the more powerful structures of the natural world. We are awed by this power over waters, wilderness and forests, and if we are wise we take note that there are allusions to human grandiosity being overcome too, the 'cedars of Libanus' being 'the great emblem of proud loftiness' in biblical poetry, as Alter puts it.[48]

The prayer connects the ideas of the voice of God with the power of God.

O God, whose voice boomed over the waters of chaos at the dawn of time, and whose call sparks magnificent flashes of lightning, drowning even the mighty roar of thunder: speak, we pray, with such compelling clarity that we may know once again the kingdom, the power, and the glory which are yours alone, and be given strength to pursue the path of peace.

The repeated return to the power of the voice of God in this psalm is an invitation to think about the qualities of a voice that make it powerful, and the uses to which a powerful voice might best be put.

---

47 Brueggemann and Bellinger, p. 147.
48 Alter, p. 99.

Psalm 30: Joy cometh in the morning

This has been described as a thanksgiving psalm, or a testimony psalm, because of the confident praise with which it begins and ends. It uses a narrative structure. In fact, two more-or-less parallel narratives – in verses 1–5 and 6–12. There is repetition here, too, which can be seen as part of the joyful exuberance of the psalmist who 'tells the story again when once does not seem enough'.[49]

Although the word 'grace' is not used here, there are parallels between this psalm and the hymn 'Amazing Grace'. Both are about being lost and then being found. The state of lost-ness is itself a product of sin and has the quality of a guilty alienation from God. This negative condition is seen as a transitional state. 'Heaviness may endure for a night : but joy cometh in the morning.' But the psalmist is not content just to let the dawn come in its own good time, seeking to move things on by petitioning God, 'Hear, O Lord, and have mercy upon me : Lord, be thou my helper.'

The psalm ends of a strong note of thanksgiving but there is no denying that it has been a difficult journey, or that it is God who is responsible for the way things have ultimately and happily worked out, 'Thou hast turned my heaviness into joy : thou hast put off my sackcloth, and girded me with gladness.'

The prayer seeks the sort of the transformation to which the psalm attests.[50]

Hear the prayers, O God, of those who recall days of deep darkness and long nights of tears. Hear the sighs of those who even now know intolerable heaviness of spirit or the crushing weight of guilt and shame. Hear the quiet groaning of all who are tormented by chronic pain. Hear them, good Lord, and bless them in their distress. Calm their souls, and raise their spirits. Replace their tears of sadness with tears of laughter; that together we may offer praise with exuberance and joy.

The contrast between 'then' and 'now' in the psalm is striking and the personal transformation is complete. Often however personal change happens slowly and incrementally and remains unfinished. What is your experience?

---

49 Goldingay, Vol. 1, p. 433.
50 This is an alternative, more personal, version of the prayer:
Hear the grateful thanks, most wonderful Lord, of this poor sinner who remembers, even now, days of deep darkness and long nights of tears; this sad soul who knew intolerable heaviness of spirit, the crushing weight of guilt and shame, and who was paralyzed by anxiety and tormented by every weakness of the flesh. Receive my thanks, O God, because all that is past: my sighs have been replaced by songs of praise, and my eyes now run with tears of laughter and joy. For a new day has dawned, and I will praise you with a spirit of exuberant and amazed jubilation, for ever, and ever, and ever.

Psalm 31: Into thy hands

This long psalm is a compilation of stock complaints, from which it is hard to discern whether there is a specific crisis behind the petitions or whether this is a more generic anthology. However, lack of originality and focus need not detract from the overall power of this extended prayer of supplication from one who is in distress and danger, or from the fresh phrases among the clichés. For instance, these words, 'Into thy hands I commend my spirit' were, according to Luke, uttered by Jesus as he died on the cross (Luke 23.46). And the whole of that verse has been used in the late-night prayer of the church for many centuries. These words still echo a feeling that we might regularly want to express in prayer, whether in an extreme crisis or as a matter of godly routine. This idea of deliberately placing the self in God's hand is echoed later in the psalm with the phrase 'My time is in thy hand.'

As in other psalms of lament and supplication, there is a spiritual uplift towards the end. In this case it might have been written after the worst was over, 'Nevertheless, thou heardest the voice of my prayer : when I cried unto thee', and in the final two verses there is encouragement to remain faithful in dark times, 'Be strong, and he shall establish your heart : all ye that put your trust in the Lord.'

The prayer is for support and restoration when isolated.[51]

> *O God, we cry to you from our places of lonely isolation. We are alienated by what we see and hear and feel, and find no fellow-feeling in our companions. Reach out to us with open hands, dear God, that we may place in them our cares, our hopes, our time, and our spirit; and guide us by those same hands into the company of your good people, that together we may grow in love for one another and be undefeated by the troubles that distress and divide us.*

The idea of placing people or events or difficulties in God's hands is clearly an ancient one, and it has had an important place in the prayer-life of many down the centuries. What do you want to place in God's hands today?

---

51 This version of the prayer is more suitable for private and personal use:
> *O God, I cry out to you from a place of lonely isolation; I am alienated by what I see and hear and feel and find no fellow-feeling in my companions. Reach out to me with open hands, dear God, that I may place in them my cares, my hopes, my time, and even my whole spirit; and guide me by those same hands into the company of your good people, that together we may grow in love for one another and for you, and be undefeated by the crises that so relentlessly assail us.*

31

Psalm 32: Thou forgavest

This psalm has an envelope structure, with the opening thoughts being reflected at the end. We find the word 'blessed' twice at the beginning, where it names the happiness that comes when the decision and practice that is narrated in the body of the psalm is recalled. The psalm ends with joyfulness and rejoicing: 'Be glad, O ye righteous, and rejoice in the Lord : and be joyful, all ye that are true of heart.' But everything hinges on what happens between, in particular in verses 3–6.

The speaker is silent. Everything is bottled up. The brilliant insight here is that this self-inflicted silence has bodily consequences. 'For while I held my tongue : my bones consumed away through my daily complaining.' If we are literally minded, we might wonder how the psalmist can engage in 'daily complaining' while remaining silent. The NRSV, however, doesn't mention 'complaining' but uses the word 'groaning', and Walter Brueggemann makes the point that a groan is 'not an intentional utterance; it is the sound of the body in anguish'.[52]

The following verse mentions another aspect of the bodily damage inflicted by this silence, 'my moisture is like the drought in summer'. Other translations use the word 'strength' where Coverdale used the more evocative 'moisture', which is apt given that dehydration literally saps our strength. The way forward? No one puts this more vividly than Eugene Peterson, 'Then I let it all out; / I said, I'll make a clean breast of my failures to Yahweh.'[53] The result is instantaneous: 'Suddenly the pressure was gone – / my guilt dissolved, / my sin disappeared.'[54]

The prayer blends a celebration of God's forgiveness with a plea for freedom from the past and for the future.

> *O God, your forgiveness is generous, quick and cleansing. Give us, we pray, the courage and honesty to speak openly when our heart is heavy with the memory of words that we regret and deeds that bring us shame. Free us from our past, we pray, and send us forward to live wisely and joyfully, trusting that there is no limit to your forgiving love.*

The insight that our body suffers when we are not able to articulate something that burdens us is an important one for our health. But what qualities do we need in order to be able to speak the painful truths that will liberate our hearts?

---

52 Walter Brueggemann, *Interrupting the Silence: God's Command to Speak Out* (Hodder and Stoughton, 2018), Ch. 3, 'Silence Kills', pp. 36–45.
53 Peterson, p. 45.
54 Peterson, p. 46.

Psalm 33: Stand in awe

It was suggested earlier that Psalm 26 is not an obviously attractive text, because of its considerable self-regard and it's not very subtle undercurrent of self-praise. By contrast, the God-facing and God-praising orientation of Psalm 33 make it warmly attractive and engaging. With its description of instrumentalists, and the suggestion that it is time to compose a new song, there is much here that can engage and energize us.

This psalm is sometimes described as a hymn, and hymn-writer Isaac Watts was among those to find a Trinitarian reference hidden in verse 6: 'By the *word* of the Lord were the heavens made : and all the hosts of them by the *breath* of his mouth.'[55]

Less controversial is the idea that the psalm seeks to paint a comprehensive picture. Although not an acrostic, its 22 lines suggest completeness by matching the length of the Hebrew alphabet. It moves from description of divine rule and governance to the invited response, 'Let all the earth fear the Lord : stand in awe of him, all ye that dwell in the world.' God is warmly praised and positively compared with creaturely or physical realities. These may impress us, but God's thoughts are incomparable, as is God's gaze; moreover his strength is of a different order to armies and cannot be compared with that of a horse.

This hymnic psalm, which began with the invitation to be thankful, ends on a note of both supplication and trust, 'Let thy merciful kindness, O Lord, be upon us : like as we do put our trust in thee.'[56]

The prayer aims to strike note of joyful praise that leads to a deeper commitment to trust in God.

> *Hear our music, O God, accept our praises, and receive all the faithful offerings that flow from our hearts in response to the excellence that we see in thy works, and the love that we know through thy word. Bless us richly, and inspire us to bless thee joyfully. And give us, we pray, the humility to place our trust in thee, that our hearts may be peaceful, and joyful, and full of hope.*

This psalm's use of images and metaphors reminds us that the psalmists were those who thought it better to say something than nothing, not those who thought they had neatly defined things or said the last word.

---

55 See Goldingay, Vol. 1, p. 473.
56 In the NRSV the final words of the psalm are 'even as we hope in you'.

Psalm 34: O taste, and see

The key to this didactic psalm is to be found in these words in verse 11, 'Come, ye children, and harken unto me.' In style it is an instructive acrostic; in content, the theme is wisdom – the sort of material that might be equally at home in the Book of Proverbs. It begins on a note of personal thanks, 'I will always give thanks unto the Lord', and invites the reader to join in: 'O praise the Lord with me', but it also encourages personal spiritual exploration; 'O taste, and see [for yourself], how gracious the Lord is.' Despite its sometimes grand and generalizing tone the psalm is steeped in experience and personal knowledge, which means that the bolder statements do not come across as bromides, but as truths won from hard experience: 'Great are the troubles of the righteous : but the Lord delivereth him out of all.'

The belief here is that God doesn't so much protect us from trouble as help us to get through the trouble that invariably afflicts us in this life and then guides us on to a far better future than we might ever have imagined. Verse 20 is quoted in John's Gospel to explain why Jesus' legs were not broken on the cross (John 19.37). The words of the final verse are of more universal relevance: 'The Lord delivereth the souls of his servants : and all they that put their trust in him shall not be destitute.'

The prayer is an expression and development of this faith.

Be with us, O God, as we seek to live well and to enjoy good days; support us as we try to be truthful and to find the path of peace, and come to our aid when our spirits are troubled. Help us to trust that in the fullness of time your grace will triumph and that the time of our tribulation will come to an end, and give us the assurance that, although we are not spared affliction, we will never be destitute.

The idea that the person who trusts in God is blessed or 'happy' expressed in verse 8 points not only to the power of God but to the power of trusting in God, but what does trust in God mean in practical terms?

Psalm 35: The great discomfort of my soul

The psalm is categorized as one of lament, and the opening 'Plead thou my cause, O Lord, with them that strive with me' references the juridical language that characterises the whole psalm. The strongest theme is 'complaint' and it grows as the psalm progresses, with the speaker first complaining about those who intend them material harm, those 'who persecute me', and then about the cynical detractors who verbally abuse, taunt and mock the speaker: 'they gnashed upon me with their teeth'. The writer is much aggrieved by this sledging, and through the psalm not only asks for God's help and salvation but prays that the perpetrators may be punished. 'Let their way be dark and slippery : and let the angel of the Lord persecute them.'

One of the surprising features of this psalm is its use of onomatopoeic words to describe the contemptuous and mocking response of the psalmist's opponents. Translators have inevitably struggled to render these into English. We find 'Fie on thee, fie on thee' in the Book of Common Prayer. Others have 'hurray, hurray',[57] 'Aha-Aha',[58] or 'Ha-ha'.[59] Also to be noted here is the sad and annoying point that although the psalmist went to the trouble of trying to help his persecutor when he fell upon hard times, 'when they were sick, I put on sackcloth, and humbled my soul with fasting' these same persecutors did not return the favour. Far from it, 'But in mine adversity they rejoiced … making mouths at me, and ceased not.' There is sore provocation here, and violent words spill from the pen of the writer throughout. It is about honesty of feeling, not intended action, and the lament is that things are not as God would order them.

The prayer seeks to reflect the emotional honesty of the psalm while remaining hopeful about eventual reconciliation.

> *Uphold me, O God, in the face of my detractors. Be my advocate, O God, before those who belittle my efforts, rejoice in my misfortunes, taunt me when I struggle, and respond to my kindness with contempt. By thy great mercy, save the weak, support the needy and turn the hearts of the cruel from the persecution of the vulnerable to the pursuit of wisdom, that weak and strong, humble and proud, may be reconciled in praise of thee.*

Expressing sadness and indignation that has been provoked by mistreatment of various kinds is one of the distinctive features of the psalms. The sentiments expressed are sometimes far from forgiving. Does this make them unworthy of us or our prayer?

---

57 Alter.
58 NRSV.
59 Peterson, p. 52 referencing, perhaps, the cartoon bully Nelson Muntz in 'The Simpsons'.

Psalm 36: The foot of pride

This psalm begins in a unique way with the personification of 'sin', or 'crime', or 'transgression'. This is sadly lost in the Book of Common Prayer, where verse 1 reads, 'My heart shewth me the wickedness of the ungodly.' The King James Version does better : 'The transgression of the wicked saith within my heart, that there is no fear of God before his eyes.' Perhaps the most evocative translation is found in the *Common Worship* Psalter, 'Sin whispers to the wicked in the depths of their heart' as it captures both the original sense of some kind of malevolent agency within, and its insidious and difficult-to-capture nature. Sin would be easier to deal with if it shouted at us in such an alarming way that it roused our defences, but the realistic suggestion here is that sin offers whispered inducements that are too subtle to recognize for what they are and too enticing to resist. However, while sin has agency within the writer, it is also active within the wicked. It is against the threat that they pose that the expansive love, mercy and righteousness of God are contrasted in verses 5–7 and 9–10.

The penultimate verse is for protection from the arrogant and ungodly, and the final verse observes the destruction that befalls the wicked. Verses 8–9 offer a beautiful picture of the refreshing nourishment that comes to those who trust God, 'thou shalt give them drink of thy pleasures, as out of the river. / For with thee is the well of life : and in thy light shall we see light', poetry that reminds us of the gentle reassurance that characterizes Psalm 23.

The prayer is for healing after we have been hurt by others.

O Lord God, whose mercy reaches to the heavens and whose faithfulness soars above the clouds, be with us, we pray, as we remember the hurts and wounds inflicted on us by those who have cravenly succumbed to temptation and who walk proudly in the way of wickedness. Replenish us with your abundant loving-kindness, for with you is the well of life, and in your light shall we see light.

This psalm points to the spiritual truth that temptation is often subtle and sin insidious, but if that's the diagnosis of our condition, what might the remedy look like?

Psalm 37: Fret not thyself

Like Psalm 34, this is a wisdom psalm. It is advisory and, like all such offerings, occasionally risks being condescending. It begins, 'Fret not thyself because of the ungodly.' Or, as Robert Alter translates, 'Do not be incensed by evildoers.'[60] A piece of advice that certainly did not shape Psalm 36.

Psalm 37 is in effect an argument, and could be considered as the obverse of the Book of Job. Job's question was, 'why do the innocent suffer?' Psalm 37 asks, 'why do the evil prosper?' Students have written endless essays in response to such questions, but this is the psalms so we don't get an essay, we get a poem, which means that the argument is based on rhetoric rather than logic.

Maybe this is part of the down-to-earthness of this genre. It is certainly not realistic to think that suffering and injustice are flicked away by a clever quip, such as, 'Yes, the evil have lots of success and plenty of fun, but it doesn't last.' That is the essence of the argument here, but much more is being expressed than that. So perhaps 'argument' is the wrong word after all. The Book of Psalms is not a piece of carefully worked reasoning but an elaboration of this line of thought, 'although we believe that in the end good will triumph over evil, it is frustrating beyond words to live with the daily recognition that evil-doers often prosper and flourish, and we struggle to come to terms with the feelings that this reality draws from us.' The focus is not on the ultimate resolution of the problem, but with the unresolved drama of living with it.

The prayer uses the language of virtue and vice to try to inhabit this conundrum in a way that reflects the whole sweep of the psalm.

> *Grant us the patience we need, good Lord, to tolerate the parade of vanity and pride that accompanies the success of the unscrupulous and the victory of the vicious. Give us the gift of humour that allows us to smile when we see the greedy gloating in their excess. Bestow upon us such a peaceable spirit that we are not troubled by the boasts of those who borrow but do not repay, and give us the courage to commit ourselves to justice, fairness and inclusion, that we, and all your people, may know peace at the last.*

Although the psalm encourages us to respond patiently when we encounter injustice, might it sometimes be appropriate that we give up on patience and allow unfairness to provoke us to action?

---

60 Alter, p. 129.

Psalm 38: Forsake me not

There are aspects of this psalm that make it familiar and others that make it strange. At 22 verses long, matching the length of the Hebrew alphabet, we might expect it to have the ambition of being comprehensive. The verses of self-blame and regret prompted the sixth-century Christian authorities to include it in the list of seven penitential psalms.[61] One distinctive feature of Psalm 38 is the causal connection between sin and suffering that is found in several places, though verse 19 provides an exception to this because here the speaker's opponents are 'without cause'.[62]

Do we imagine that the psalm was written in real time by someone suffering, or by a sympathetic observer reflecting later? Scholars differ in their answers but to many readers the ambiguity might be helpful; we could read it in either way depending on whether we are suffering ourselves or compassionately engaging with the suffering of a friend.

Although it has an envelope structure, Psalm 38 has no element of 'closure'; the ending and beginning are a plea to God from a place of personal suffering. The difference is that while at the beginning the plea is to be spared angry rebuke, at the end it is the cry not to be forsaken. Maybe that's spiritual progress enough for one psalm.

The prayer is a personal one that comes from a place of chronic suffering.[63]

Why this suffering, O God? Why this burning pain? Why this frustration? Why this loneliness? Why this interminable ticking of meaningless time? Are you angry? Have I done wrong? Do I need to grovel in penitence for my sins? What do you want of me? Answer me clearly, for as yet I hear nothing. I see nothing. I am consumed by my own suffering. Does this please you? It pleases my opponents. You have done their work for them. Now I will do whatever is needed to find favour in your sight, to find release from this suffering. Come to my aid, O God, forsake me no longer. Tell me what to do.

This is one of many psalms that can deepen our understanding of the experience of suffering. However, might it be wise to accept that though we may try we will never fully understand the suffering of others?

---

61 See the comment on Psalm 6 for a list of penitential psalms.

62 NRSV. This nuance of translation cannot be found in Coverdale's version, which rather unhelpfully focuses on the quantitative 'they that hate me wrongfully are many in number'.

63 I am thinking of those who suffer from conditions such as Locked in Syndrome and degenerative conditions such as Multiple Sclerosis, Parkinson's Disease, or Motor Neuron Disease (ALS), and those at the early stages of progressive dementias, such as Alzheimer's.

Psalm 39: Let me know mine end

This short psalm is clearly one of prayer and petition, but it doesn't take the typical form and doesn't seem to be a response to a specific problem or crisis. Rather it brings to the surface the ambiguities of ongoing life. It's a psalm about life's grey areas and uncertainties and the tenuous nature of our grip on truth, hope and faith. The penultimate verse reads, 'For I am a stranger with thee', and the final verse suggests that there is an undergirding existential crisis that it not yet resolved, 'O spare me a little, that I may recover my strength : before I go hence, and be no more seen.' This theme of mortality is strong in the second part of the psalm, which modulates from the bursting desire to know more about how and when life will end to the worry that living itself is 'vanity', that is, without meaning or worthwhile purpose. The psalm mentions hope, but in this case hope doesn't overcome uncertainty and anxiety.

The psalm also has an interesting and realistic dialectic between speech and silence. It begins with the commitment to 'keep my mouth as it were with a bridle', but a few verses later there is a real outburst, 'Lord, let me know mine end.' Later again, silence returns, 'I became dumb, and opened not my mouth', though not for long. Before the psalm ends God is asked to recognize that the tears being shed are a kind of prayer, 'hold not thy peace at my tears'. The final verse does not come across as well as it might in Coverdale's version, the poetic 'O spare me a little, that I may recover my strength' is rendered in the NRSV as ' Turn your gaze away from me, that I may smile again' and Alter has 'that I may catch my breath'.[64] Coverdale's final half verse is also a little coy; to be 'no more seen' is a watering down of the total obliteration that is in fact imagined and articulated by the writer.

The prayer is an expression of fundamental anxiety.

Hear my prayer, O God, for I come before you rendered helpless by anxiety that will not be resolved by the wise words of others, or careful thoughts of my own. My life – I want to know how it will progress and when it might end. My purpose – I want to know my calling and to be confident about my priorities. My hope – I want to know what I might reasonably expect in this world and the next. I am drifting, and long to come closer to your truth and your love. Restore in me the confident faith of my younger days before I lose all sense of your presence.

This psalm takes us shockingly close to the prospect of our own complete non-existence and insignificance. Dare we accept the message that in prayer we really may imagine the worst before God?

---

64 In the NRSV this is verse 13 and in Alter it is verse 14.

Psalm 40: My heart failed me

Coverdale's translation of the opening of Psalm 40, 'I waited patiently for the Lord and he inclined unto me', does not adequately communicate the urgency of the waiting or the intensity of the hope that lie behind this psalm. In his paraphrase, Eugene Peterson makes the point by repetition, 'I waited and waited and waited for Yahweh. At last he looked; finally he listened.'[65] God not only listened but responded, rescuing the speaker from 'the horrible pit, out of the mire and clay' and placing them upon a solid rock where there is firm footing. Verse 3 declares that 'he hath put a new song in my mouth', and the next that, seeing this wondrous transformation, many 'shall put their trust in the Lord'.

This in turn leads to a beatitude: 'Blessed is the man that hath set his hope in the Lord : and turned not unto the proud, and to such as go about with lies.' The psalm then turns to further celebration of God's goodness, and ponders what an appropriate human response might be. Moments of lamentation emerge as the psalm goes on, reversing the normal psalmic pattern in which lamentation leads to thanksgiving.

The psalm concludes with a puzzle, because the final few verses make up the whole of Psalm 70. So which came first? Psalm 70, in which case Psalm 40 is an expanded version of 70. Or 40? In which case, 70 is an edited form of 40. Unsurprisingly, scholarly views about this differ. The final verse repeats the opening sentiment. The psalmist is tired of waiting, 'make no long tarrying, O my God'.

The prayer recapitulates the opening verses of the psalm, imagining the swamp from which we need to be rescued as the product of our own mistakes.

Hear our prayer, O God, which rises this day from the miry swamp of our many mistakes. Free us from the quicksand of complacency that so dangerously entraps us. Pull us to safety, and set our feet on solid ground, that we may walk in your way, embrace your will and sing your praise.

What is the emotional impact of such an ancient expression of impatience? Is it encouraging to know that our forebears were impatient, or is it rather dispiriting to discover that impatience has a very long history?

---

65 Peterson, p. 59.

Psalm 41: Heal my soul

This psalm brings to an end the First Book of Psalms[66] and in some ways reflects the psalm with which the whole collection began, Psalm 1. Both, for instance, begin with a beatitude. In Psalm 1 the happy person 'delights in the law of the Lord', in Psalm 41 the happy person has considered 'the poor and needy'. Where they differ most significantly is that Psalm 41, like most of the intervening psalms, is alert to the way in which things often go wrong in life. It lists various circumstances that could easily put an end to any personal happiness. It suggests that part of the antidote to this is to take an interest in the lives of others and to care about their misfortune.

Careful reading clarifies that Psalm 41 doesn't proclaim the blessedness of the poor *per se*, as do the beatitudes in Luke's Gospel (Luke 6.20–23). The blessedness, or happiness, which is declared and celebrated here, is of the person who has *considered* the poor, noticed them, thought about them, had compassion on them and taken some action for or with them.

The prayer is for faith-based resilience.

Help us, O God, to retain our faith and our integrity when things go against us, and secure our confidence when people speak ill of us or betray our trust. Keep us ever mindful of our own need for mercy and forgiveness, but let us never be bullied or humiliated because our conscience is weak. Rather, return us to the path of compassionate care and righteous action, that we may enjoy your blessing, and rejoice in your enduring love.

The obvious challenge of this psalm is to reflect on our attitude towards the vulnerable. It can't be right to be condescending or patronizing, but what *is* the right attitude to have towards the poor and needy?

---

66 See above, p. xv.

Psalms 42 and 43: (A) My soul is athirst

The repetition of the same refrain in both Psalms 42 and 43 is reason enough to consider them to be one psalm. And the theory is reinforced by the fact that the theme of 'yearning for God' spans the two. It's also worth noting that not only does this psalm begin the Second Book of Psalms, but that the word translated 'God' here is not the name 'Yahweh', which has been used in Book One, but 'Elohim'.[67]

This God, Elohim, is mentioned very many times in these verses, not because God is palpably present to the poet, but precisely because God is absent and longed-for.

While Psalm 22 begins with the absence of God and moves on to a celebration of God's presence, Psalm 42/43 sustains the spirit of unrequited longing with which it so memorably begins to the end. This psalm doesn't resolve. It is an expression of yearning for God, not finding God. And therein lies its spiritual power; something perhaps made particularly evident in Herbert Howells' anthem 'Like as the Hart', which is a setting of verses 1–3.

The prayer is that God would meet us in our yearning.

Receive, O God, not only our songs of praise, but also our deepest desires and our most urgent and profound longings. Meet us, we pray, in the honesty of our yearning, that we may know the consolation of thy love and have the patience to wait for the peace that passes all understanding.

We live in a world where the prompt achievement, fulfilment and satisfaction of desire is highly prized, but the suggestion here is that it is the quality of our longing that matters more.

---

67 See above, pp. xvii–xix.

Psalms 42 and 43 (B): Thy waves and storms

The imagery of water in diverse forms is important in Psalm 42. We encounter, the 'water-brooks' (v.1), the tears that 'have been my meat day and night' (v.3), and then the great crashing waters, memorably, but most unhelpfully, rendered by Miles Coverdale as 'the noise of the water-pipes' (v.9).

But this image is not about plumbing, it is about the destructive power of chaos. Translators have struggled here. So in various versions we read of 'the thunder of your cataracts',[68] or 'the sound of your channels',[69] or even 'the tune of your whitewater rapids'.[70] The second half of the verse gets a more unanimous translation: it's about the surf. We are to imagine breakers and waves overwhelming the inundated individual. Once we appreciate that the phrase with which the verse begins 'One deep calleth another' can be rendered 'chaos calls to chaos', we can see that this is not about submarine calm, but about churning, noisy, confusion and a sense that we are at the mercy of great powers. These may be malevolent, benevolent or random; we just can't tell. It doesn't matter, as we are in the middle of it all and can see no way out.

The prayer is an attempt to connect with our primal fear in the face of chaos.

> *Attend, O God, to those who are disoriented by chaos. Rescue all who are lost in confusion. Count the tears of those who whisper their prayers in the lonely watches of the night. And by thy great goodness, hear us when we cry out to thee: reassure us and make us safe.*

If we have experienced a storm at sea, we will know its impact on our faith and our prayers both in the moment and in the calm that followed. If we have no such experience then this psalm offers an opportunity to the imagination.

---

68 NRSV.
69 Alter.
70 Peterson.

Psalm 44: Lord, why sleepest thou?

The word 'lament' is not powerful enough to describe the middle section (verses 10–22) of Psalm 44. A defeat of some kind has been suffered, and is experienced as betrayal. God has abandoned the people, let them down and, not only are they defeated, but humiliated and mocked. It is the blunt tone of the protest that is so striking: 'thou lettest us be eaten up like sheep', and 'Thou makest us to be rebuked of our neighbours : to be laughed to scorn, and had in derision of them that are round about us.'

God seems to have abandoned the people, but it becomes clear in verse 19 that they have not forgotten God, 'Our heart is not turned back : neither our steps gone out of thy way.'

The psalm ends with a cry to God to act, which is less of a plea, and more of an instruction mingled with a rebuke, 'Up, Lord, why sleepest thou : awake and be not absent from us forever' and, finally, 'Arise, and help us : and deliver us for thy mercy's sake.'

The prayer is for victims of the powerful, reflecting some of the urgency of the psalm.

> O God, your forsaken people cry out from places of desperation, defeat and despair. Hear their cry, and come to the aid of all who are abused and crushed, ridiculed and mocked by those whose power is unbridled. Rise up! For your tender mercy's sake, deliver the suffering, the exploited and the oppressed from every kind of evil.

The psalms bring many negative experiences to God, among them disappointment and betrayal, and they do so with great honesty and articulated urgency. This could be depressing, but might it also be a liberation?

Psalm 45: A ready writer

This is the only psalm to begin with an expression of the enthusiasm and energy of a psalmist as wordsmith: 'My tongue is the pen : of a ready writer.' This might help explain the fact that this psalm, which seems to be a poem to celebrate the king's marriage to a foreign bride, is not only unique among the psalms in being a song of praise to a person, rather than to God, but that it is the king who is described as God – not God as a king.

This is not apparent in every translation, including the Book of Common Prayer. At issue is verse 7: 'Thy seat, O God, endureth for ever : the sceptre of thy kingdom is a right sceptre.' Robert Alter has such translations in mind when he writes: 'Some construe the Hebrew here to mean "Your throne, O God", but it would be anomalous to have an address to God in the middle of the poem because the entire psalm is directed to the king or to his bride.'[71] Although this reading makes the psalm theologically problematic, it does have integrity; the poet really is praising the actual king and groom as if God.

The prayer is for those who will shortly celebrate marriage.

Pour thy blessings, O God, on those who will soon be married in this place. Shower them with gifts and graces. Anoint them with gladness. Surround them with loyal friends, and give them long life. Strengthen them in truthfulness, justice and humility that their name may be highly regarded, their home a palace of hospitality and their influence good and far-reaching.

It is interesting that the prospect of a happy wedding ceremony generates such energy and enthusiasm in the poet. What occasions tend to stimulate your loquacity?

---

71 Alter, p. 159.

Psalm 46: Be still

This well-known psalm is rich with imagery and contrast. Its 11 verses draw together the most extreme sense of threat with the most profound call to peace. The first point is that although the very foundations of the planet are disturbed, there is no cause for fear. The hills that 'are carried into the midst of the sea' are better understood as the mythical pillars of the earth within the oceans, on which the whole planet is set. If they wobble, everything wobbles; if they crash, everything crashes. The oceanic waters are threatening and chaotic, they 'rage and swell'. In the original Hebrew there is alliteration, which might even suggest a degree of seasickness.[72] But then there is a pause.

Verse 4 also has water, but it is the water that shall 'make glad the city of God'. There is no river in Jerusalem apart from an underground stream, but that is beside the point. Water here represents divine mediation and refreshment. The emphasis turns now to the strength of the Lord of hosts, literally 'God of the armies', who is 'with us' (see verses 7 and 11). For those who want the psalm to be about peace, and it does indeed end in peace, the apparent method of achieving it, the out-gunning of military powers, is somewhat paradoxical and is an awkward embarrassment for those who believe that ends can never justify means.

What is encouraged here, however, is not the taking up of arms but reliance on the Lord of hosts and the God of Jacob. And so we are invited to 'Be still then, and know that I am God.'

The prayer is for peace in our hearts and in our world.

Give us the strength we need, O God, to be fearless in the face of threat and to be hopeful when there are no grounds for hope. Settle us when we resonate with the shaking of the cosmos or the quavering of the fearful. Help us to listen for your voice when surrounded by the noise of battle or deafened by the anxious beating of our own heart. Renew our sense of your abiding presence, release us from vain attempts to control the uncontrollable, and establish in us the poise and purpose of your all-encompassing love.

The instruction to be still is a rather unusual one in today's world, and yet it is one that many people long to hear. Stillness matters. The challenge, perhaps, is to model it; to be still yourself.

---

72 Alter quotes the Hebrew and translates it to emphasize the alliteration: so 'yehemu yehmeru meymaw' becomes 'the waters rage and roil'.

Psalm 47: A merry noise

One way to contrast this psalm with the previous one is in terms of noise. In Psalm 46 the noise was threatening. In Psalm 47 the noise is joyful and celebratory and much encouraged. Blow a trumpet by all means, but there is no need for skilful or beautiful music – and the notion that songs should be sung 'with understanding' is not replicated in more accurate translations, which simply want the singing to be joyful or plentiful. It's exuberance that is wanted here, not excellence.

There are some who believe that this psalm reads more like 'rubrics', the words of instruction you find in a service book; that it is a description of a liturgy in which God is enthroned as king, not the words of the service itself. Whether or not this is plausible or true,[73] we are now reading it as a psalm among psalms, and that involves recognizing that, even if it was once a set of ritual notes, it became *content* a very long time ago. Someone was inspired to see the meaning in these words, even if they were first written down as a set of instructions.

The ultimate kingship of God is a strong theme. God is both the God of Israel and of all peoples, 'God reigneth over the heathen.' This theological totalitarianism leaves no scope for plurality and puts all other claims, indeed all other gods, very much in their place. Emphasizing the sovereignty of God in this way affirms that God has first claim on our loyalty, and that there is no limit to the relevance of our faith, or the scope of faithful action. If the God who is monarch were not a God of truth and loving-kindness, this would be very worrying indeed. But since it is the God of truth and loving-kindness who is king our response is not anxiety but praise.

The prayer encourages exuberance before the one true God.

O King of all the earth, your loving-kindness and truth pervade the cosmos and call us to obedient and joyful living; hear us as we praise you with all our heart, with all our voice, and with all our strength. Hear us as we clap our hands. Hear us as we stamp our feet. And hear us as we sound a fanfare. O God, O king, O ruler of all, accept our praise, and let your peace be known in all places.

This psalm challenges us to reimagine politics in the light of a theology that understands God to be both a peaceful king and also a liberating friend of the poor and needy.

---

73 Robert Alter does not believe any such ceremony ever took place, Alter, p. xvi.

Psalm 48: In the midst of thy temple

There is an uncomfortable element of theological boasting in this psalm: 'Our God is great and lives in the temple in the most beautiful and fortified city imaginable. If you don't believe me, come and take a look!' So it prompts us to ask whether there can ever be a form of boasting that is healthy. The issue here is perhaps similar to the point about kingship in the previous psalm. Although grandiose claims can be unhelpful, ultimately self-falsifying and even corrupting, if they happen to be true, they should be made with absolute conviction. Nonetheless, the danger of overstatement remains. Is Jerusalem really impregnable? Or is it, in fact, just so beautiful and impressive that its destruction is not so much unlikely as unbearable and therefore unimaginable?

There is also a conversation to be had about the kind of presence that God has in the temple. This psalm could be read in parallel with 1 Kings 8, where the peripatetic God is transferred to the stable dignity of the holy of holies. This is not to capture or to limit God, but to give reassurance and comfort to God's people and provide a focus to their devotions. This suggests a helpful way of engaging with this psalm, and turns us to the verbs of sound and sight in verse 7. 'Like as we have *heard*, so have we *seen* in the city of the Lord of hosts, in the city of our God : God upholdeth the same for ever.'

The grandiosity is significantly reduced by the time we get to verse 8, which has a calmly contemplative tone. 'We wait for thy loving-kindness, O God, in the midst of thy temple.' It is this humble but hopeful *waiting* for God that is at the centre of the psalm; and it is rightly at the centre of the temple, the city, the nation, and, if you will, the world.

The prayer is that we may be drawn into transformative prayer.

Draw us, O God, to the calming mystery of your presence, that we may enter more deeply into the wonder of your love, ponder more profoundly its implications for our lives, and witness more adequately to your grace, your glory and your goodness.

This psalm draws us to a deeper consideration of the nature of the presence of God and its implications for us. Might it be that when we are aware of God we feel less need to be in control and less need to rush?

Psalm 49: Wise men also die

This is a wisdom psalm, which, like others we have seen already, has a didactic tone and is addressed to the reader rather than to God. The writer is confident that they have an important message that everyone needs to hear. Namely, that what passes for wisdom is often seen to be folly when placed in the context of our mortality. In verse 10 we read that 'Wise men also die.' This may read like so much common sense, but people are all too often sucked-in by vain fantasies of quasi-immortality: 'And yet they think that their houses shall continue for ever : and that their dwelling places shall endure from one generation to another; and call the lands after their own names.'

I recall having to suppress a wry smile when reading this psalm at evening prayer when a curate in Greater Manchester. The parish is officially named as St John the Divine, Baguley, but it is always referred to as St John the Divine, *Brooklands*. This is because the neighbourhood is called 'Brooklands' after the nineteenth-century businessman Samuel Brooks, who brought the land from the Earl of Stamford and built himself a large house on what became Brooklands Road, and on which the parish church now rather proudly stands. It seemed to me that Mr Brooks had actually achieved something worthwhile in his life and that there was affection and appreciation in the use of his name. Maybe the psalmist was overstating the point.

Nonetheless there is a danger to us of envying those whose success in life is rewarded by fame or by them having 'a name', even if few today would aspire to having that name inscribed into the local geography. The bigger truth is that those who prosper or become famous come to the same end as the rest of us. The writer wants us to see worldly advantage and status against the more distant horizon of God's future. It's when we take this view that we can respond wisely to the successes and achievements of others.

The prayer is for freedom from envy.

Deliver us, O God, from the envy that so often afflicts us when we behold the achievements and privileges of others. Take from us the mean-spiritedness that resents the rewards that they reap. Turn our attention to the blessings we enjoy and the pleasures of our own life, and, as we remember the constraints and limits of this life, guide us to the contemplation of the true joy of your endless love.

The question of what we will leave behind us is one that we rarely discuss. Given that you probably won't be giving your name to a neighborhood, building or project, what would you like your legacy to be?

Psalm 50: A consuming fire

After an introduction of praise the Psalm is made up of two prophetic oracles. The first begins at verse 6 and addresses those who offer sacrifices but with the wrong motivation. It is a matter of 'covenant', which is a deeper matter than 'contract', connecting the heart and the mind, and where mutual regard and care, one might even say 'love', are important. Without this level of engagement, religious actions, even spectacular sacrifices, are meaningless. Indeed, excessive emphasis on doing the right thing only makes matters worse, as it reveals the absence of deeper respect and relationship.

The second oracle begins in verse 16 where it is the 'ungodly' who are addressed. These are those who do not even try to do the right thing. They keep bad company, speak bad words, and completely forget God and the Ten Commandments. The 'wicked' here are keeping bad company, speaking bad words, forgetting God and the basis of the divine-human covenant, as summarised in the Ten Commandments. Psalm 50 calls time on this sort of negligence. People may think that God hasn't noticed, but God has indeed noticed. Unworthy, inadequate and wrongheaded actions will certainly have consequences. You may have forgotten God, but God has not forgotten you!

The first half of Coverdale's translation of the final verse clarifies that it is thanks that God desires, and not sacrifice. The second half is easier to understand in more contemporary versions. These do not use the word conversation but refer to the right way, that is of living life as a whole.

The prayer is for the integration of faith and life.

Rebuke us, O God, when we fail to regard others with care and affection. Disrupt our religion when it lacks humanity or warmth. And make us once again mindful of your deep desire for our love, and your utter disregard of our anxious efforts to win your favour.

The challenge of this psalm might be to be honest about which of the two warnings is most relevant to us – the warning about being superficial in our religion or the warning about being negligent in our ethics.

Psalm 51: A troubled spirit

The heading or superscription to Psalm 51 is perhaps the most vivid introduction of any, 'To the leader. A Psalm of David, when the prophet Nathan came to him after he had gone in to Bathsheba.'[74] The Latin version of this psalm was most famously set to music by Gregorio Allegri (1582–1642). Known to millions as 'Allegri's Miserere', it is often sung on Ash Wednesday and Good Friday. But the point at issue in the psalm is not a general one about the sort of sinfulness we feel when in the presence of holiness, but the very specific sin of contriving and executing an adulterous plan.

Some commentators suggest that this is actually a much later psalm that has been retrofitted to this situation, citing in particular the way in which the psalm reflects the theology of later prophets and the reference to the rebuilding of the walls of Jerusalem – something not relevant at the time of David. Such scholarship need not stand between us and a bold spiritual reading of the psalm for ourselves; even if it is actually retrofitted to the story of David and Bathsheba, the fit is very good. Questions of authorship and date matter much less than the question of what the words actually express and how that expression informs the faith of those who read or recite these words.

The prayer is a plea for forgiveness and the opportunity to make a fresh start.

Most merciful God, we come before you mindful of your mercy and goodness and of the depth of our sin and the seriousness of our transgression. We do not seek to hide our guilt or disguise our shame, but to reveal how we have lost our way and hurt others. Receive, we pray, this offering of a crumbling self, and forgive us our sins. Make something new of the broken mess that we have become, that we may live well, offer praise, and, in the fullness of time, help others to find their way to your forgiveness and peace.

In Psalm 51 the sense of alienation from God mingles with a deep desire for God, which is, perhaps, a reality for many people today. The psalm's power is that it takes seriously the impact of genuine guilt on the sinner.

---

74 NRSV. The story of David and Bathsheba is told in full in 2 Samuel 11 and 12.

Psalm 52: A green olive-tree

This psalm begins by addressing an anti-hero, 'Why boastest thou thyself, thou tyrant : that thou canst do mischief?' Although God's goodness persists, this hubristic antagonist plots destruction, catastrophe and disaster, speaks deceitfully and pursues the ways of evil, regardless of the harm caused. There is a particular focus on the use of malicious words, 'Thou has loved to speak all words that may do hurt : O thou false tongue.'[75] The psalmist responds to this threat by asserting that God will not tolerate this interminably. Robert Alter translates this with dramatic words, 'God surely will smash you forever, / sweep you up and tear you from the tent, / root you out from the land of the living.'[76]

The contrast is then set up. The anti-hero trusts not in God but in money and power, '[this is the man that] trusted unto the multitude of his riches, and strengthened himself in wickedness'. The speaker in the psalm is deliberately different: 'As for me, I am like a green olive-tree in the house of God : my trust is in the tender mercy of God for ever and ever.' The peace-implying picture of an olive tree rooted in the soil of God's own house suggests humble, good and godly living that is in vivid contrast to the way of the tyrant.

The prayer is for those who are subject to hurtful words and damaging gossip.

Remember, O Lord, all who have been slandered or subjected to denigrating gossip. Send them sympathetic supporters, and companions who might restore their spirits. Bless us all with a spirit of kindness, that we may always see the good in others, and speak well of our friends, colleagues and neighbours.

This psalm reminds us that our attitude and outlook is not always personally chosen but can be a product of our experiences. And yet we do not need to remain victims of our experience and can, perhaps, become kinder as we get older.

---

75 Some other translations refer to 'all words that devour' (NRSV), 'destructive words' (Alter) and 'malicious gossip' (Peterson).
76 Alter, p. 185.

Psalm 53: Where no fear was

Although this psalm is largely a reproduction of Psalm 14, there are some subtle differences that suggest a new and important focus for prayer. Psalm 14 is concerned with the poor whereas Psalm 53, like Psalm 52, gives more attention to the 'abominable', or 'perverse': the word used in verse 4 to describe those who do not believe that God will hold them to account.

Verse 6 is also a clear point of difference. Many commentators mention that the beginning of the verse is difficult to translate. Coverdale's 'They were afraid where no fear was' is a good approximation if one believes Alter's contemporary approach. He translates as: 'There did they sorely fear/ – There was no fear', and comments that 'There was no fear.' The least constrained way to construe this clause, which does not appear in Psalm 14, is as implying, 'but' 'They [presumably the Israelites] were afraid, but it turned out that there was no reason to fear.'[77]

The prayer seeks to connect with this experience of pervasive fear without a cause.

> *O God, my heart knows fear, my soul knows fear, my mind knows fear, and my strength and my calm have gone. I am deeply anxious. Rekindle my faith, and inspire me with fresh hope, that I may live with confidence once again.*

Fear without obvious cause, or anxiety, is rife today. But anxiety must also have causes. Where should we look for the causes of the anxiety that so many people experience today?

---

77 Alter, p. 188.

Psalm 54: God is my helper

According to tradition, this psalm derives from the occasion when David was hiding from Saul.[78] David can be considered as 'the representative person of faith struggling with the perils of life, especially with enemies'.[79] This is not an unusual topic in the psalms, and nor is it an uncommon human reality. Life is rarely a sunny stroll in the park. It's more often like trudging across a boggy moor in the mist.

The particular perils that this psalm highlights are encounters with threatening others, referred to here as 'strangers' and 'tyrants'. Different translators and commentators have used various other designations, and the reader can choose between words such as '[the] insolent' and '[the] ruthless',[80] or 'strangers' and 'oppressors',[81] or 'willful people' and 'terrifying people',[82] or even 'outlaws' and 'hit men'.[83]

The prayer is the personal petition of someone who has walked into danger.

> *O God I am in trouble; urgent, deep and desperate trouble. I have displeased powerful people and they are intent on causing me pain and on ruining my prospects. This is new for me. I am frightened. I am not able to cope. I need protection. Save me, O God.*

Psalm 54 reminds us that the terrain of life's journey is difficult and perhaps even dangerous to traverse. When we understand this, the question is how we become courageous enough to move forward.

---

78 See 1 Samuel 23.15–17.
79 Brueggemann and Bellinger, p. 248.
80 Both NRSV.
81 Both Alter.
82 Both Goldingay.
83 Both Peterson.

Psalm 55: My companion

This psalm is perhaps better known for the musical setting of a few verses than for the whole piece. In the nineteenth century, Felix Mendelssohn (1809–47) was asked to set verses 1–6 as a piece for solo, choir and orchestra.[84] Yet powerful as the words of the opening verses are, with its profound sense of longing so sympathetically captured by Mendelssohn, 'Hear my Prayer' does not exhaust the spiritual treasury that is Psalm 55.

In particular, the psalm includes the report of a personal betrayal, the sort of experience that for some people might resonate with the most difficult experience of their life. No one is likely to set *these* verses to music, but Coverdale's words pack a poetic punch that more recent translations don't quite convey. 'For it is not an open enemy, that hath done me this dishonour : for then I could have borne it. / Neither was it mine adversary, that did magnify himself against me : for then peradventure I could have hid myself from him. / But it was even thou, my companion : my guide, mine own familiar friend.' Verse 22 adds to the picture: 'The words of his mouth were softer than butter, having war in his heart : his words were smoother than oil, and yet be they very swords.' The sense of betrayal is crushing, the feeling of disappointment complete. Friends are the people whom we choose in the belief that they will not let us down. So where are we to turn when they do just that? The advice quickly follows, 'O cast thy burden upon the Lord, and he shall nourish thee : and shall not suffer the righteous to fall for ever.'

The prayer is for those who have been betrayed.

Look kindly, O Lord, on all those who are desolate at heart because they have been betrayed by a friend or loved one. Be with them as they experience new depths of disappointment. Protect them when overcome by rage, and shield them from the corrosive forces of self-blame. Give them the strength to endure their pain, embrace them with your life-giving love and give them abundantly of your restorative spirit.

One of the strengths of literature is that it invites us to imagine the unthinkable. And yet it is hard to find anything in literature that has not happened to someone, and which not might one day, happen to us.

---

84 Interestingly, he was sent the words in English but translated them into German himself, keeping the stress and the syllable count as similar as possible. As a result, 'Hear My Prayer' has been sung in both German and in English since about 1855–56.

Psalm 56: I am sometime afraid

Like Psalms 54 and 55 this can be categorized as a psalm of lament, but it is also a prayer for protection that combines alternating statements of fear and trust. It begins, 'Be merciful to me, O God.' This is 'merciful' in the sense of 'gracious'; not 'forgiving'. The speaker's trouble is caused by others and they are afraid because of the threat that they pose, not as a result of their own actions. What is most interesting about the psalm is the way in which fear abruptly moves to trust and trust cancels out fear. Henry Purcell put two of the verses to music in the seventeenth century, 'In God's word will I rejoice : in the Lord's word will I comfort me. / Yea, in God have I put my trust : I will not be afraid what man can do unto me.' The music reflects the joyful nature of the utterance, which is, in fact, a refrain – appearing first in a slightly different form in verse 4. So perhaps this psalm could be read through the lens of joy rather than that of lament. This is certainly the feeling that Purcell's setting conveys.

There is another strong theme too, which is a twist on the idea of lament. This is expressed in a beautiful image in which God is closely attentive to the poet's distress. 'Thou tellest all my flittings; put my tears into thy bottle : are not these things noted in thy book?' The idea is that God counts as meaningful, and remembers, all the troubles that have been experienced and from this counting – a metaphor for taking note, noticing, acknowledging – it is understood that everything shall be redeemed.

The prayer is of joyful praise and expresses thanks for past deliverance.

We rejoice in your gracious love and eternal compassion, good Lord, for you have regarded our suffering, felt for our pain and counted our tears. We rejoice in the faith which has been a rock in times of trial, and a refuge when we have been afraid. We rejoice that you have brought us back from the brink of mortal danger and pray that you will guide our feet into the way of life and peace, trust and joy.

Often, we apologize when we have let our feelings show that we are troubled, but might the recognition of the depth our distress or sadness sometimes be necessary for healing to begin?

Psalm 57: My heart is fixed

There are several familiar features in this psalm. For instance, it begins in the same way as Psalm 56, except that in this case the speaker's trust is mentioned first. It is this trust that makes the psalmist confident that they will survive the current 'tyranny'.[85] Slightly later the difficulties caused by others are mentioned. In this case the trouble seems to be in the form of malicious words rather than mortal threat: 'And I lie even among the children of men, that are set on fire : whose teeth are spears and arrows, and their tongue a sharp sword.' The experience of the speaker is of being hunted, but the power of God is evident when the hunter eventually falls into his own trap.

A positive, settled and praise-filled tone emerges throughout and comes to fulfilment in the final verses. These words appear again later in the Psalter where, with only very minor changes, they comprise the opening verses of Psalm 108. They read very differently, however, as the conclusion rather than the opening of a psalm – there is an implicit 'therefore' at the beginning of verse 8: '[Therefore] my heart is fixed, O God, my heart is fixed : [and so] I will sing, and give praise.'

The prayer is for those who are sheltering from dangers of all kinds.

O God, whose steadfast love reaches up to the heavens and fills the whole earth, look with mercy upon all who are sheltering from danger, whether the threat is to their physical life or their mental health, whether it comes from the natural world or from the mouths of the malicious, and give us, and all your people, the faith, the confidence and the energy to rise each day with your praise on our lips and the vision of your glory set before our eyes.

The question of trust is an important theme across the extraordinary wide range of experiences depicted in the Book of Psalms. It seems that belief and trust go hand in hand. Indeed, can we really say we believe if we do not trust?

---

85 The NRSV doesn't have 'tyranny' but 'destroying storms'.

Psalm 58: Break their teeth

This psalm is so dangerously filled with the desire for vengeance, and with vividly imagined consequences for evildoers, that the whole thing is often deemed inappropriate for public use. The focus is on the ungodly – the callously wicked who will halt at nothing to achieve their goals. However, it is not their intentions or methods that get the greatest attention here, but the writer's desire that God will deliver a crushing retribution. It is this that distinguishes Psalm 58 from the many others in this part of the Psalter that are concerned with the power of enemies and those with destructive or evil intent. 'Break their teeth, O God, in their mouths; smite the jaw-bones of the lions, O Lord : let them fall away like water that runneth apace; and when they shoot their arrows let them be rooted out.' Make no mistake, the writer here really does want to see the wicked suffer: 'The righteous shall rejoice when he seeth the vengeance : he shall wash his footsteps in the blood of the ungodly.'

The desire is to be able to conclude, on the basis of having seen such vengeance, that 'doubtless there is a God that judgeth the earth'. But who are the wicked? It's really difficult to be sure because the Hebrew of this psalm is both 'mangled and crabbed'.[86] However, Alter uses the word 'chieftains' in the first verse, suggesting that the wicked being referred to here are leaders, people in positions of authority and responsibility. The NRSV calls them 'gods' and Coverdale used the phrase 'sons of men'. Whoever they are, the psalmist is clearly extremely angry at their abuse of power.

The prayer is for a situation in which power has been abused.

Hear, O God, the depth of our disappointment and the strength of our anger when we learn that those in positions of trust and power have exploited and abused the vulnerable. Accept, we pray, our deep indignation and our burning rage. Comfort and console those who have been harmed and change the hearts and minds of those who have served themselves at the expense of others, that our community may be healed and that we may come to enjoy the blessings of mutual respect and peaceful relationships.

This psalm insists that we recognize the enormity of the damage done to society and to individuals by those who have abused their power and invites us to question any response that does not recognize the harm inflicted on victims of such abuse.

---

86 Alter, p. 202.

Psalm 59: God of my refuge

This is a very angry psalm in which vivid language is used to vent feelings. It begins in an unremarkable way with a petition to be saved from enemies, but after a couple of verses the writer warms to the theme. 'For lo, they lie waiting for my soul : the mighty men are gathered against me, without any offence or fault of me, O Lord.' The psalmist is energized by the unreasonableness of the situation, and this seems to fuel his verbal inventiveness. 'They go to and fro in the evening : they grin like a dog, and run about through the city.' The notion of the dogs 'grinning' might imply a smirk of schadenfreude, unconcealed delight in another's suffering, but other translations opt for words like 'howling', 'growling' or 'muttering' – which suggest that gossip is part of the mix. In any case, we can be sure that the writer is emboldened by their indignation; 'dogs' is such a very pejorative term in the Hebrew context that to use it at all is audacious.

This boldness extends also to the way in which God is addressed. God is not quite instructed here, but God is certainly told what it is that a God worth their divine salt would do in such circumstances. The detail of this changes somewhat from verse to verse, the inconsistency being perhaps an indication of the emotional state of the writer – who in anger wants contradictory things by way of punishment.

Spiritually and psychologically it seems to work. By the end of the psalm the writer is in a place of peaceful confidence, 'Unto thee, O my strength, will I sing : for thou, O God, art my refuge, and my merciful God.'

The prayer follows the method of the psalm in naming trouble and seeking peace.

Save us, O God, from those whose hostility and unkindness threaten us, and hear our prayer as we complain about those who are cruel in their intentions towards us, those who lie to us, those who mock and humiliate us and those who deprecate and curse us. Give us confidence, strength of mind and wisdom that, knowing your peace and rejoicing in your love, we may overcome all the hatred and hostility that others can direct at us.

No one knows whether they would be bold enough to turn to prayer when faced with raw hatred until they see it in someone's eyes or hear it in their voice. Nonetheless the psalms give us a great example of how to pray when life is deeply difficult.

Psalm 60: Vain is the help of man

Psalm 60 begins by lamenting the woeful state of God's people in a situation that is experienced as divine rejection: 'O God, thou hast cast us out, and scattered us abroad.' As becomes clear towards the end of the psalm, the feeling here is one of bewildered sadness that there was once a time, but it is now sadly passed, when God acted and God's people were free.

In the middle of the psalm, verses 6–8, we find a divine oracle, an announcement of God's promise in the past, which was fulfilled and, as a result, the people came to prosper. These words, which are repeated verbatim in Psalm 108, speak of the expansion and consolidation of the tribes of Israel – Gilead, Manasseh, Ephraim and Judah. But the blessing and support for some is balanced by the ejection of others, 'Moab is my wash-pot; over Edom will I cast out my shoe.'

The rhetoric is strong here, but, unlike the previous psalm, we cannot say that the rhetoric is the point; that the psalm works as a prayer because it is a transformative vehicle for powerful feelings. This psalm is one that engages the transformative power not of rhetoric, but of memory. The reminder is that the people really do have a special place in God's heart.

The way in which the psalm ends is both curious and ambiguous. It is not entirely clear that the divine support remembered and promised is forthcoming after all. Nonetheless, the last verse is positive, even if the triumph here is one of historic memory over present experience: 'Through God we will do great acts : for it is he that shall tread down our enemies.' For clarity it might be honest to add, 'or so we have been led to believe. So here's hoping'.

The prayer is that God will be loyal to us when we turn in prayer for support and strength.

Turn our hearts and minds, O God, from their anxious concern about recent troubles to the recollection of the great days in the past when we were confident of your love and protection. Rekindle in us the gifts of faith and hope, that we may overcome our troubles and serve your purposes.

This psalm sees memory as an anchor in reality that gives rise to genuine hope. When memory is less healthy it nostalgically draws us backwards. Nonetheless, when it is remembered well, the past can help us prepare for the future.

Psalm 61: The covering of thy wings

This short psalm begins in desperate petition and ends in praise and commitment. The speaker does not spell out the problem, trial or adversity, nor are the details of the suffering clarified. Confidence in God's ability to provide what is needed is expressed in terms of various metaphors: the rock, the strong tower, the 'tabernacle' or tent, the shelter under God's own wings. An important clue comes early on, 'From the ends of the earth will I call upon thee : when my heart is in heaviness.' The writer is distant and alienated; caught somewhere in the shadowlands between life and death.

This psalm may have been written as a prayer for the king's long life, see verses 6–7, but some scholars believe these verses to be a later, somewhat intrusive, addition. Whether or not this is the case, there is no reason to narrow the scope of a psalm that can be relevant to all who are entering their last days or hours.

The prayer is for those who seek reassurance as they approach death.

Hear the quiet call, O God, of those now approaching the end of their days. Give them calm, give them peace, and give them the company and care they need. Bless them with the satisfaction of good memories, and take from them all heaviness of heart, that their soul might be strengthened as their bodily strength fades away. Be for the dying, O God, a strong rock, a high tower and a dwelling place of abiding security and peace. Cover them with the shadow of thy wings, and enfold them in the constancy of thy loving-kindness, for thy tender mercies' sake.[87]

In today's world it is easier to forget that we will all die than it would have been at any other time in history, and so the prospect of our own death can seem shocking to us. What might help us to get beyond the shock and towards healthy acceptance?

---

87 The final two sentences could be used as a prayer on their own.

Psalm 62: In God is my health

This is a psalm of patience and trust in God in testing circumstances. It begins, 'My soul truely waiteth still upon God : for of him cometh my salvation.' And quickly clarifies that this is not the idealized waiting of trouble-free meditation in a beautiful place, but a determined act of resilience in the face of adversity. The writer is beset by those whose 'delight is in lies', and those who 'give good words with their mouth, but curse with their heart'. There is recognition of having been misled and the poet is now ruing the consequences of being so gullible. But this writer is not going to give up, 'Nevertheless, my soul, wait thou still upon God : for my hope is in him.'

God is the foundation of the writer's trust and the reader or listener is enjoined to follow that example. 'O put your trust in him always, ye people : pour out your hearts before him, for God is our hope.' The word 'hope' perhaps has a somewhat abstract ring, and might be a bit ethereal to someone in real trouble. The original is more concrete and has been translated 'refuge' or 'shelter'.[88]

Ultimately it is the second part of verse 11 that carries the burden of this psalm: 'power belongeth unto God'. This is the basis of real trust and genuine hope; it is the surety of the place of refuge, and the reason that patient waiting is appropriate.

The prayer is for faith, trust and calm in the most difficult of circumstances.

Give us the faith, O God of our strength and our salvation, to put all our trust in your power and your love. Give us a true and deep sense of the vast expanses of time that you have made. Enable us to wait on you with patient calm and in the peaceful hope and lively expectation that your kingdom will come, and that the problems that we are faced with will be resolved in your good and gracious time.

We encounter once again the theme of trust, and are reminded that it is when trust is most difficult that it is most real. And yet true deep spiritual trust cannot be the same as gullibility. The question is how we distinguish deep trust and sheer gullibility.

---

88 The NRSV has 'refuge' and Alter has 'shelter'.

Psalm 63: My soul thirsteth

As it was in the previous two psalms, trust is a strong theme in Psalm 63. It begins, however, with a profound sense of longing – as if God, while trusted, is absent and missed. This is a very different kind of absence than is experienced and expressed in various other psalms, such as Psalm 22 where the absence of God is a desperate or bitter reality. This psalm has more of the feel of the opening verse of Psalm 42, 'Like as the hart desireth the water-brooks : so longeth my soul after thee, O God.' This is especially clear in verse 2: 'My soul thirsteth for thee, my flesh also longeth after thee : in a barren and dry land where no water is.' But even this desert experience is juxtaposed to a positive experience of God. Verse 3 concerns not only longing for God, but looking for God, 'Thus have I looked for thee in holiness : that I might behold thy power and glory.'[89]

The second part of the psalm, verses 5–9, is a short master-class in practical spirituality. There is recognition of the deep satisfaction, 'even as it were with marrow and fatness' that is the result of praise. Then there is the idea of nighttime meditation, the recollection of help in the past, and the joy of feeling under the shadow of the divine wings, and, at last, the idea of the soul clinging to God: 'My soul hangeth upon thee.'

The final verses turn to the less personal issues of the ultimate destiny of aggressors and enemies, and the triumphant vindication of the king.

The prayer is that the desires and longings of our hearts may be met by God's grace.

Be with us, gracious Lord, as we sing thy praises in the company of your people, and as in solitude we meditate on your goodness through the silent hours of the night. Keep us under the shadow of your wings, and uphold us as we reach out to you, longing for nothing more than to know your divine kindness and to give voice to your praise with a glad song on our lips.

The beautiful blend of trust and longing in this psalm takes us to the root of our prayer and spirituality, which might sometimes be expressed as patient longing and other times as active seeking. Both are good, but which do you find more natural?

---

89 'In holiness' here does not refer to the attitude of the writer but the place where they are looking – other translators, use, words such as 'sanctuary'. For instance, the NRSV has 'So I have looked upon you in the sanctuary, / beholding your power and glory.'

Psalm 64: The imagine wickedness

This is a psalm that recognizes the destructive power of language and the peril in which we can be placed by the talk of others. As verses 2 and 3 make clear, there is a dangerous noise abroad. It is the sound of tongues being used as swords or arrows. Speech itself is being weaponized. Contemporary readers need no reminding that this ancient phenomenon has not yet burnt itself out. There are many occasions today when the power of language to hurt and harm is deployed.

A turning point comes in verse 7, where the hunting metaphor is reversed. Those who have weaponized words find that they have been playing with fire: 'Yea, their own tongues shall make them fall.' Ironically, it is this that people will start to talk about, 'And all men that shall see it shall say, This hath God done : for they shall perceive that it is his work.' Or, as the NRSV has it, 'Then everyone will fear; / they will tell what God has brought about, / and ponder what he has done.'

The psalm concludes with a verse of rejoicing.

The prayer expresses the desire to speak helpfully when hostile words have been spoken.

Hear the voice of our quiet prayer, O God, and grant that by speaking kindly and carefully we may invite your healing grace into the noise and chaos of this troubled world.

The power of language is all too obvious in the psalms; more easily overlooked is the impact, intended and unintended, of our own choice of words and the tone of our voice.

Psalm 65: The madness of the people

Scholars tell us that the behind the words at the opening of this psalm lies the idea that God is praised in silence.[90] Such a notion is difficult to express in words, obviously, but is worth bearing in mind as this poem careers on its way from this opening sense of great mystery to the wonderful relishing in the abundant fruitfulness of creation that emerges later on.

This is a very positive psalm indeed, brimming with words of thanksgiving and with images to delight the heart. In the eighteenth century Maurice Green made a charming and encouraging motet of the first half of verses 9 and 12: 'Thou visitest the earth and blessest it ... and crowneth the year with thy goodness.' Much more recently, in 1989, David Willcocks set the whole psalm to music in his *Ceremony of Psalms*. He too brings the vibrant and positive part of the psalm to life as it progresses, but not before dwelling extensively on this more difficult verse. 'My misdeeds prevail against me : O be thou merciful unto our sins.' A salutary reminder, perhaps, that we cannot appreciate the beauty and abundance of the created world, and that we will we not see it participating in the active praise of God, as the final verses suggest, unless and until we can get over our self-concerns.

The prayer seeks to reflect the joy of the psalm.

Open our eyes, O God, that we may see the wonders of this world, and cleanse our hearts that we may appreciate its beauty with renewed gratitude; and by your great and abiding goodness, visit and bless this earth, that we may sing your praise with joyful songs.

On our best days we are aware of beauty and life all around us, on our worst days we just don't notice it. Might it sometimes be the case that it is our self-concern that prevents us enjoying this life?

---

90 Alter translates the opening verse: 'To You silence is praise, God, in Zion, / and to You will a vow be paid.'

Psalm 66: Behold the works of God

This is another very positive psalm. It starts with the widest possible invitation to be joyful, 'O be joyful in God, *all ye lands*' and 'For all the world shall worship thee.' The writer is energetic in describing their own actions, ' I will go into thine house with burnt-offerings : and will pay thee my vows ...' and 'I will offer unto thee fat burnt sacrifices ...' while offering invitations, or even instruction, to others to be joyful and give thanks.

Every now and again the writer seeks to draw the reader in more closely. For instance, 'O come hither, and behold the works of God : how wonderful he is in his doing toward the children of men', which leads to a catalogue of recollected wonders. Later there is a similar invitation, but what is disclosed is more personal, 'O come hither, and harken, all ye that fear God : and I will tell you what he hath done for my soul.'

The psalmist then speaks of their own prayer-life and testifies that God does indeed hear and 'consider' these personal prayers. There is no mention of them being 'answered', but there is satisfaction enough in the understanding that the prayer has not been 'cast out' and that God's mercy has not been turned away.

The prayer offers praise and asks God to continue to bless us.

We praise thee, O God, with joyful hearts; for thy providence has provided for us, thy power has delivered us and thy loving arms hold us in life. Accept our praises, receive our prayers and continue to touch our souls with thy grace, that we may ever receive thy blessings and come to know thy glory.

Our prayers are sometimes effortless, sometimes full of tension, sometimes heavy with request, and sometimes joyful. This psalm seems to invite us to reflect on what we hope to achieve by praying. But maybe 'achieve' not quite the right word ...

Psalm 67: Bless us

The upbeat tone of this part of the Psalter continues in Psalm 67, which combines a warm sense of personal blessing with a positive view of the created world. The benediction at the beginning reflects the great blessing of Aaron in the Book of Numbers (Numbers 6.24–26), in some ways making it even more expansive, 'God be merciful unto *us* and bless *us.*' Indeed there are no limits in this short psalm, 'Let the peoples praise thee, O God : yea let *all* the people praise thee' and, 'God shall bless us : and *all the ends of the world* shall fear him.' If it is felt that the word 'fear' strikes a negative tone at the end, it might be noted that more recent translations use words like 'revere'. God is admired and praised as saviour and guide, and, as in Psalm 65, the earth is seen as giving abundantly.

This is a psalm that reflects good days, the harmonious times when people enjoy peace and prosperity, and it can hardly fail to communicate deeply felt joy when read or sung today.

The prayer reflects the psalm's sense of expansive and transformative praise.

> *Open our hearts, O God, that we may glimpse your glory and know your grace. Fill us with joy and let all peoples rejoice with us. Let the earth be fruitful, and teach us how to express our reverence for you and respect for each other.*

In reading and praying this psalm we are exposing ourselves to the contagion of joy. There can be no certainty of outcome, but a real risk is that we may find ourselves profoundly happy.

Psalm 68: The earth shook

The 35 verses of this psalm take the reader on an emotional journey that begins with the plea, 'Let God arise.' It then remembers at length the times in the past when God has indeed arisen, together with the consequences for those against whom God arose, before moving on to offer a new plea that God will be active today. It ends with a final shout, 'blessed be God'. Whether it was composed as one piece or complied from existing poems or fragments of poetry is a question that many scholars have asked. The reality for us is that it is presented as one whole psalm, and we are challenged to make sense of it both in its components and as a whole.

A question we might well ask is how we can make the journey from the petition that God will arise to the acclamation 'blessed be God!' It is unlikely that people today would expect to narrate the history of recent wars as part of that, and we would certainly not expect to describe in positive detail the casualties of the action (see verses 21–23), nor would we think to describe in such a narrative the intricacies of a liturgical procession or celebratory parade as are detailed in verses 24 and 25. Our world, our experiences, our expectations and our values do not always seem close to those of the psalms, and yet we do know what it is to want God to be more evident to us, and we do believe that there is truth as well as desire and hope in the acclamation, 'blessed be God'. The question is how we live in the space between.

The prayer is an acclamation of God's goodness.

Blessed be thou, O God, for thy care and protection of us thy people in this place. We praise thee for the grace that has so often gone before us, and for thy loving responses to our prayers. We thank thee for the occasions when we have had a powerful sense of thy presence among us and when we have experienced the joy of glimpsing thy glory and knowing thy grace. Blessed be thou, O God.

The goodness of God is something we take for granted when we offer praise, but it is seriously questioned when we reflect on human suffering. The question might not be which comes first, praise or theological reflection, but which comes last.

Psalm 69: I wept

This 37-verse psalm is the extended prayer of someone who is suffering innocently, very probably at the hands of religious opponents. It oscillates between plea or petition, on the one hand, and protest or complaint, on the other.[91] In fact there is a great deal of complaining in this psalm, which culminates in robust petition that those whom the speaker deems to be responsible for their suffering, or for aggravating it, will have even worse suffering inflicted on them. These vengeful sentiments can be embarrassing to witness and the words are uncomfortable to recite. The psalm doesn't end on this note, however; the final verses are rich with trust and praise.

The prayer is for those who are indeed angry about their own suffering and passionate for justice.

Hear the prayers, O God, of all who are overwhelmed by trouble, oppression or persecution. Hear them as they call to you in their distress and their anger, and hear us as we pray for justice for the downtrodden, vindication for the misunderstood and restoration of the dignity of the falsely accused. Hear, O God, the prayers of the poor. Hear, good Lord, the voice of the oppressed. Give ear, O holy One, to the pleas of the tortured, and by your great mercy, bring all their suffering to an end.

We can be deeply troubled by our own feelings of vengeance, but feeling bad about feelings doesn't make them go away. This psalm provides an opportunity for us to accept any unresolved vengeance in our heart, and to pray ourselves beyond it.

---

91 Compare verse 1a (plea) with verses 1b–5 (complaint); and verse 6 (plea) with verses 7–12 (complaint).

Psalm 70: Haste thee unto me

This brief psalm has been thought of as a 'sigh'.[92] Its verses are also found within Psalm 40.13–17. There are slight differences in wording, not least that in Psalm 40 it is the name 'Yahweh' that is used, whereas here it is the word 'Elohim'.[93] The background to the psalm is not a specific event or circumstance but the overarching covenant between God and God's people.

The fact that Psalm 70 doesn't seem to derive from or belong to any particular context is perhaps what makes it feel applicable in a wide variety of different but difficult circumstances. The speaker is having a bad time. The cause, it seems, is unspecified others. God is asked to sort it all out by punishing the persecutors and blessing the poor. Some believe that these verses were originally found alone, so that Psalm 70 is original and Psalm 40 is a later development.

The prayer is a short and direct petition to God in time of need and disorientation.

> *O God, thou great redeemer, thou merciful deliverer, thou champion of the needy: look upon us, understand our condition, and make haste to come to our help, that we may once again be joyful and glad in thee.*

The idea that a psalm can be a sigh reminds us that sometimes in our prayer we reach the limits of language before God. It might be suggested that never to have encountered that limit is never to have prayed ...

---

92 H. J. Kraus makes this suggestion, quoted by Brueggemann and Bellinger, p. 304.
93 These different words are typical of Books One and Two respectively. See Introduction p. xvii.

Psalm 71: When I am grey headed

This psalm contains so many familiar psalmic phrases that some have suggested that it is in fact a compilation of already existing verses, carefully arranged as a pulse beat of alternating petitions and trust-statements. This use of existing material is perhaps consistent with the suggestion that it is the personal prayer of someone who is well advanced in years, whether middle-aged with many more years of life to come or knowingly approaching the end of their days.

The speaker is certainly aware of the ageing process and the ambiguities of the passage of time, 'O what great troubles and adversities hast thou showed me, and yet didst thou turn and refresh me : yea, and broughtest me from the deep of the earth again.' Acute awareness of the ambiguities of ageing is the distinctive gift of this psalm.

This prayer holds before God some of the thoughts of those aware of ageing.

The years go by, dear Lord, my store of memories swells, and the reasons for regret, or doubt or distress increase. As I become older, I am ever more aware of the frailty of my flesh and find myself increasingly anxious about the future. Bless me, I pray, with a renewed sense of your protection, heal the memories that still cause me pain, and kindle in me the gift of hope for the future, that I may sing your praise with the integrity of my years.

We live in a culture where youth is valued over age and yet where life expectancy is greater than it has ever been. Might this suggest that the virtue we will most need in the future will not be wisdom but humility?

Psalm 72: Deliver the poor

This psalm is about leadership. In particular the royal leadership of King Solomon, who prayed for wisdom but nevertheless left quite a mess behind him. What is most interesting about the psalm is that it doesn't begin with prayers for the king's health, wealth and happiness – though it does come around to these later – rather the prayer is primarily that the king might reflect the justice of God, both in his person and in the use of his power. This is the priority – a just and fair society in which the interests of the weak and vulnerable are given serious attention. If the king's reign reflects and realizes such values, then he will indeed be a good king and there will be every reason for praying for a lengthy and successful reign. This psalm conveys and emphasizes the imperative of justice and care; the recognition that all people matter equally to God is not just a thought here, but a basis for ethical action.

The final two verses are not really part of this psalm but serve the purpose of bringing the Second Book of Psalms to a suitable ending.

The prayer is for political leaders today.

O God of peace and wisdom, give your blessing to those who offer political leadership today. May their words be honest and true; may their deeds be kind and caring; may their minds be open to criticism and their hearts be open to correction; and may their legacy be of equality, inclusion and justice for all people.

One of the great struggles that has shaped western politics is between social justice and personal freedom. Does our faith encourage us to engage with, seek to undermine or transcend this dynamic?

Psalm 73: I was grieved at the wicked

This is a psalm about *almost* going astray; it is about vulnerability to a certain kind of temptation and sin. It begins blamelessly, the writer knows what's what and expresses it succinctly in the first verse, 'Truly God is loving unto Israel : even unto such as are of a clean heart.' The pure in heart are good and God responds to them. This is understood, but the writer is an honest person and goes further, 'Nevertheless, my feet were almost gone : my treadings had well-nigh slipt.' Why? Then comes a confession that we can all relate to, on some days with closer affinity than others: 'I was grieved at the wicked : I do also see the ungodly in such prosperity.' And so it goes on. The writer really is very distressed at how well other people seem to be doing; at how success comes to those who are far from being pure in heart.

The writer is experiencing a form of dispiritedness based on envy, and it is almost, but not quite, overwhelming. Verse 12 shows that the writer gets to the brink of capitulating to these ugly feelings but then stops, understanding that the consequences of going any further would be grave.

What follows is a combination of thought and prayer. The poor writer is wracking their brains, but it is too difficult for thought alone and gets 'stuck', as schoolchildren say in their maths lessons when the problems are too difficult. As is often the case, a change of context liberates the mind and imagination. So our psalmist is only stuck, 'Until I went into the sanctuary of God : then understood I the end of these men.'

What follows is the recognition that success, prosperity, worldly power and the like do not last. There is a timescale and context that makes them irrelevant. True fulfilment is found in other ways and over the longer term. Faith and praise are better than envy. Not only are they better for mental health purposes, as we might say today, but they are more realistic and true.

The prayer is that we may not be drawn into envy but remain faithful and humble.

Save us, we pray, Lord God, from the envy that besets us when we see the prosperity of others. Save us from the feelings of resentment that arise when we observe that the arrogant and rude are successful, and when the wealthy please themselves and corrupt those who look to them for example. Give us, we pray, the grace and wisdom not to be troubled by the sins of others, and keep us faithful to the path of righteousness, truth and humility that will lead us, in the fullness of time, to your eternal and righteous kingdom.

This psalm's attitude towards envy may be contrasted with the attitude towards anger and indignation in other psalms. Anger is to be worked through whereas envy is to be overcome. Might this be because there is often sometimes a positive reason for anger whereas envy is always negative?

Psalm 74: The King of old

Like Psalm 68, Psalm 74 is a prayer that God will arise. The structure is different, however. It begins with a lament about the absence of God, and goes on to list the evils that the enemy has done, taking advantage of this absence of God and causing havoc, not least in 'thy sanctuary'. The historical context is the destruction of the temple in 587/6 BCE. This is a much greater symbolic tragedy than, say, the fire at Notre Dame in April 2019 both because it was intentional destruction and because the temple was an even more potent symbol, being viewed as the centre of life and hope; indeed as the centre of the universe itself.

The psalm then moves into the mode of remembering what God did in the past. The turning point comes in verse 13: 'For God is my King of old : the help that is done upon earth he doeth it himself.' There follows a litany of great acts of God recalled from various times in the past but with a strong emphasis on the calming of water and sea monsters – symbols of energetic and hostile chaos.

Finally, God is invited to notice what is going on in the here and now and get involved in sorting it out. This really is God's business as well as the concern of the writer. Phrases such as, 'maintain thine *own* cause' and, the concluding words, 'the presumption of them that hate thee increaseth ever more and more' make it clear that the suffering of the psalmist is paralleled by the offence caused to God.

The prayer seeks to turn nostalgic sentiments into forward-looking hope.

O God, the king of old, look upon the trouble that faces your people today. So much that we have built up has been destroyed; so much that we value is derided; so much that speaks to us of your love and power is mocked. We fear the arrogance of those who oppose all that our faith means to us and tremble as we see the forces of chaos and anarchy gather and swell. O God, the King of old, hear our prayer above the roar of the chaos, and by your abiding mercy, return us to the peace of your calm, the beauty of true worship and the confidence of strong faith.

The absence of God is a deeper and more troubling feeling than that of longing for God. It is difficult to live with and made desperate when we can remember a time when God seemed close. But an absent God is not a nonexistent God, and prayer remains real.

Psalm 75: God the Judge

Like Psalms 73 and 74, this psalm is concerned with God's order in the face of the arrogance of hostile others. Psalm 75 is the shortest of the three and can be difficult to follow because the voice changes quite abruptly. It opens as a prayer of thanksgiving, but in verse 3 it is God who is speaking. In biblical poetry, the 'horn', mentioned in verses 5 and 6, is a common image for arrogant self-assertion.[94] The writer then responds in verse 7 and continues to the end, but using a variety of styles.

At the heart of the psalm are two related ideas. It is God who will steady a tottering world and it is God who judges all. People are unsettled, faith is difficult, things don't seem to be working out … these are the observations and feelings that impel the writer to write. And yet they do not lead to despair but to faith and renewed confidence. The imagery of the last verse is vivid, 'All the horns of the ungodly also will I break : and the horns of the righteous shall be exalted.' But this is not random or meaningless violence, or even the violence of revenge. It is the arrogance of the arrogant that will be destroyed. This needs to happen so that the genuine pride and honour of the virtuous can be recognized and respected. The faith here is that under God, justice will win through. Life is ultimately fair and we are on a journey towards good order.

The prayer is for reassurance and calm.

Give us the faith, O God, to trust in the constancy of your grace when we are unsettled by the arrogance of others and when we fear for the stability of our society. Reassure us when we are anxious. Calm us when distressed. Strengthen us when we are close to capitulating to despair, and give us the patience to leave the judgement of others to your wisdom.

By giving sustained attention to the theme of human arrogance the psalmists invite us first to interrogate responses to the arrogance of others with informed honesty and, second, to reflect on why arrogance is such a profound spiritual error.

---

94 See Alter, p. 262.

Psalm 76: The earth trembled / Thou art to be feared

This psalm is a celebration of God's power and of God's work. It praises the God of Jerusalem who is strong and secure, who is able to see off and subdue the mightiest and most fearsome of enemies, and whose righteousness extends to justice and equality for 'all the meek upon earth'. The 'meek' in this case are not those of a virtuously humble disposition; rather they are the oppressed, the poor, the defeated and the subjected. Read with this knowledge, the psalm is a great source of encouragement to liberation theologians, and it has been suggested that such texts as this have found their fruition in the Helsinki Universal Declaration of Human Rights in 1948.[95]

In this psalm, God is a loyal and good friend of the poor. God will not let the rich and powerful have their way. God is not content with exploitation. God is not content with gross inequality. God can, and will, act in ways that the proud and arrogant find invincible: 'Thou, even thou art to be feared : and who may stand in thy sight when thou art angry?' The ending confirms the same point: 'He shall refrain the spirit of princes : and is wonderful among the kings of the earth.' If anything, this translation is too soft and more recent translations have phrases like 'He plucks the life-breath of princes'[96] and 'inspires fear in the kings of the earth'.[97]

The prayer is for liberation of the poor and oppressed.

Hear our prayer, most holy God, for the dignity and equality of all peoples of the earth. Be with all who struggle for their own human rights and for those who fight for the rights of others, and by your mighty power subdue those who would subdue your people. Come forth with justice, O God, that the poor and oppressed may know the joys of freedom and peace.

This psalm tells us where God stands, and confronts us with the question of whether we side with the oppressed or the oppressor.

---

95 Brueggemann and Bellinger, p. 330.
96 Alter, p. 267.
97 NRSV.

Psalm 77: My own infirmity

There is a hinge, or pivot, in this psalm. Up to verse 10 it is the voice of difficult and perhaps depressed experience that is most apparent. After verse 10 we hear the more confident and positive affirmations of the voice of faith. The writer is in reflective mode throughout. There are many references to remembering, but those opening verses of realism are important in two ways. First, for their honesty. The writer here is not at ease, in particular they are not sleeping, they have too much on their mind. In conversation they are tongue-tied, and not at all confident that their troubles will end. Life is bleak indeed. A lesser religion, a lesser document of faith, would simply erase all this material and give its energies to positive thinking and generating an attractive yet ultimately superficial feel-good factor.

Second, there would also be something lesser in focusing only on the approach and experience of the first half of the psalm. There *is* progression here, which we might think of as a dialogue that moves forward. Reality and faith, experience and hope, do not drift apart in this psalm. They challenge each other and thereby lead to a wise maturity of outlook, which in turn fashions the remarkable attitude of faith and trust mentioned in the penultimate verse: 'Thy way is in the sea, and thy paths in the great waters : and thy footsteps are not known.' God is to be followed despite the danger inherent in doing so, and despite the fact that God leaves no footsteps to guide us.

The prayer is for those whose troubles disturb their sleep.

Be present, O God, to all those who seek you in the quiet hours of the night. Although their voices are silent, hear the pleading of their hearts and the longing of their souls. Touch their minds with calming thoughts, help them recollect their most reassuring of memories and bless them with faith, trust and rest.

The experience of restlessness is neither comfortable nor satisfactory. It can have many causes but ultimately feeds on itself. Faith is perhaps the ultimate answer, but what is it about faith that generates calm, acceptance and peace?

Psalm 78: Marvellous things

Lengthy and dramatic, this psalm is a repository of the history of God's people that was probably always intended for recitation in public as a reminder to the elders and as a lesson for the young. There is a strong 'never forget' element to it: never forget the Exodus from Egypt, never forget the wandering through the desert, never forget that the Exodus wasn't easy; never forget that God is powerful and on our side.

But there is another 'never forget' too. Our ancestors were favoured, but they were not always as faithful or as trusting in God as they should have been. Unaccountably, they wouldn't trust the liberating God to be a providing God, and they were always inclined to make their own gods, to put their trust in idols.

This in turn leads to more 'never forgets'. Never forget that God notices the unfaithfulness, the lack of trust, and the idolatry, and that God never forgets the rage they provoke. However, God's wrath doesn't lead to the people's destruction, but to yet more blessings – manna in the wilderness, for instance. And yet the story from there is not one of God's unequivocal blessing and grateful human response. It is much more stormy than that. From time to time the people understand and repent – if a little half-heartedly – and God is compassionate and merciful and recognizes that human beings are inevitably frail, that they are 'but flesh'. Nonetheless, if only they had remembered the plagues inflicted on Egypt, and if only they remembered now what happened to those who practice false religion, they might do better. And so these stories too are narrated.

All of which leads on to the final 'never forget': that while all this did indeed provoke the wrath of God, who oversaw the punishment of the people at the hands of their adversaries, in the end God is roused once again to defend the people, effectively forgiving them. God then offers them a new future under the chosen King David.

The prayer is that we should never forget.

O God of all time, let our hearts and minds ever be open to the lessons of history, that we may tell with honesty, candour and insight the stories of the past, and never forget the mistakes of our ancestors or the power of your passion for justice and faithfulness.

This psalm might be seen as an anti-nostalgia manifesto, and it invites us to reflect on the extent to which it would be healthy and helpful today for us to be more realistic about the mistakes and failures of former generations.

Psalm 79: Where is God?

This sad and angry psalm has as its context the Babylonian destruction of Jerusalem and the temple. This is vividly described. Jerusalem is 'a heap of stones' and 'The dead bodies of thy servants have they given to be meat unto the fowls of the air : and the flesh of thy saints unto the beasts of the land.' More than a national disaster, this was a catastrophe for faith and of hope. The city had survived the attacks of the Assyrians and was understood to be inviolable. It is not surprising, therefore, to find that verses 1–5 are laden with complaint.

These are followed by a series of petitions – requests that God comes to the help of the desolate people and, if this is all punishment for sin, that God should consider it to be punishment enough. 'O remember not our old sins, but have mercy upon us, and that soon : for we are come to great misery.' After all, this is not only bad for the people; it is bad for their God's reputation, 'Wherefore do the heathen say : where is now their God?' The petition extends into a desire for retribution meted out on the invaders and the promise of renewed and eternal thanks – when freedom and dignity have been restored.

The prayer is for those who have suffered invasion.

Hear, O God, the cries of people whose homes and cities have been conquered, whose holy places have been defiled, and who have been humiliated at the hands of invaders. Be present with all who know the degradation of defeat, and with people who have witnessed the torture or murder of family members. Bear with all who seek liberation, and those who desire revenge, and give your healing grace to all who turn to you as they seek freedom and dignity for the generations yet to come.

There is a clear challenge here to try to imagine what it might be like to try to survive in a city that has been invaded or overrun. When struggling with this it might be a further challenge to remember that for too many people this is not a theoretical exercise.

Psalm 80: Turn us again

This psalm has a refrain that recurs three times: near the beginning, towards the middle and at the end: 'Turn us again, O God : show the light of thy countenance and we shall be whole.' Implicit in it is the whole story of the psalm. The people are under threat and in danger. They feel this is because they are alienated from God, or perhaps wrongly oriented. They need to turn or to be reconnected and then see again the shining face of God. If they achieve this then all will be well.

God, it is thought, must be angry. Tears are their food and drink and, to add insult to injury, they are locally derided: 'Thou hast made us a very strife unto our neighbours : and our enemies laugh us to scorn.'[98]

This is a communal lament, but maybe we can relate to it at a personal or domestic level. There are times when everything seems to go wrong. All that has been built up over the years seems fragile or precarious, and then, perhaps suddenly, the extent of our losses overwhelms us, our friends desert us (or we them) and we are the butt of cruel comments. This is when we need to be reassured in the deepest possible way. This is when we want God to gaze upon us with loving eyes. This is when we need to see God's face.

The prayer is for those who feel that God is distant.

Hear our prayer, O good and kindly shepherd, and look upon us in this time of loss and threat. We mourn the good days of the past. We resent the mockery of our critics. We fear the intentions of our enemies. Return to us again, O God, show us your face and restore us to wholeness, integrity and joy.

This psalm encourages us to turn to God not only when we have wilfully turned away from God ourselves, but just as importantly when we have been disoriented by forces that are more powerful than we are.

---

98 The NRSV has the blander 'our enemies laugh among themselves' and Alter the economic 'our enemies mock us', p. 285. Peterson says that they 'poke fun at us', p. 116.

Psalm 81: Sing we merrily

This psalm begins on an appositive note of joy, 'Sing we merrily unto God our strength.' An ad hoc orchestra is gathered so that a joyful noise in praise of God can be made. It is to be in harmony with the universe and the passing of time. It's good to celebrate the new moon, with, if the sky is cloudless at night, surprising and ethereal light. There is enjoyment here and celebration. William Byrd's anthem 'Sing Joyfully' reflects the happiness and exuberance of these verses. God has done well for the people and will do well for them in the future.

Sadly, however, that's not the whole psalm. In fact, that part of the psalm ends halfway through verse 5, though this is impossible to appreciate from the Prayer Book version where the words 'and had heard a strange language' seems to refer to the speech of the Egyptians. But this is a misreading. These words introduce all that follows, which is a divine oracle, and so they are better translated, 'I heard a voice I had not known.'

The oracle, which should perhaps be in speech marks, is in two parts; the first of which recounts historical events while the second takes the people to task for deciding not to listen to God. There is a significant emphasis on listening here, or 'harkening' as the Prayer Book has it. The people were blessed, but didn't listen; they were given a route map, but chose to take a different journey. No anger follows on this occasion. God is sad rather than wrathful. The final part of the oracle is, as it were, a divine lament. The people have prevented God helping them as God would desire. This is folly and sadness.

The prayer reflects the opening of the psalm and is for a celebratory festival.

On this festal day, our worship sounds out your praise. Yet we fail in our response if we do not heed your voice or obey your word in our actions. As we open our hearts to feel the joy of your love, open our ears that we might hear your voice, and open our minds that we may understand your word, obey your will and follow your way in all we do.

There are perhaps many reasons why we might not listen to God, but is it joy or sadness that most distracts us from this contemplative task?

Psalm 82: A Judge among gods

Psalm 82 imagines a scene and a series of events that are somewhat off the map of life and faith as we know it today. It posits a trial between the various gods of a polytheistic universe. It is not necessary to inhabit that strange cosmology to be inspired by the psalm, however. Verse 2 puts the question on the table, 'how long will injustice prevail?'[99] The question doesn't get a direct answer. The trial's judge turns straight to instruction, making it clear that justice isn't achieved by pontificating about ideals but that it is result of certain actions. The poor and orphans are to be defended, the needy are to be provided for, the outcasts are to be rehabilitated and all those vulnerable to being exploited are to be protected from the unscrupulous. Here we see the deep origins of the vital connection between monotheism and social justice.

In the verses that follow the lesser gods are deprecated, 'They will not be learned nor understand, but walk on still in darkness.' The consequences of this are dire and general; they are not only bad for the victims of injustice. This is an important point. When power is used badly 'all the foundations of the earth are out of course'. Verses 6 and 7 suggest that there is genuine learning here. The 'gods' or 'princes' or even 'judges' seemed at one time to have divine status, but now they are understood to be lesser beings both ontologically and ethically. In the final verse a new speaker prays that the one true and universal God will take charge, 'Arise, O God, and judge thou the earth.'

The prayer is for social justice.

O God of justice, strengthen all who desire to see a world of fairness and equality, and inspire us to adopt the attitudes, and take the actions, that will improve life for the poor, the outcast and the needy. Protect, we pray, the vulnerable from those who would exploit them or who would compound their suffering with further oppression, and deliver us all from the snares of corruption, that together we may know the joy of freedom and equity.

Polytheism may seem very remote from contemporary secular humanism, but might there be some fundamental similarities?

---

99 This is the NRSV translation. Coverdale's is 'How long will ye give wrong judgement?'

Psalm 83: Keep not still silence

Those who have never been under serious threat, or have managed to forget what real threat is like, will find it hard to connect with Psalm 83. Imagine that everything that you have come to take for granted, all that you rely on, every aspect of life that gives you comfort, and all the people you love, are in danger of being destroyed. Now you are at one with the writer of the psalm, and you will know and feel that the idea of a God who is above the fray and who keeps 'still silence' is intolerable.

Under existential threat the need is not for a God of calm and restraint, but of action. The causes of this profound threat do not need to be understood or accepted, but to be dealt with in the same way that existential threats have been dealt with in the past. The predators need to be blown away as fast and as far as possible, even as they make their plans to move in and destroy our homes.

The fantastical image in verse 13 'O my God, make them like unto a wheel' is simply a poor translation. Think rather of 'whirling dust'[100] or even 'thistledown'.[101] Put alongside the desire for a firestorm to push the enemy back, it is clear that there are very strong words here, expressing equally strong feelings. They are overstatements made from a place of deep and desperate anxiety. They are worthy not because they express graciousness but because they have the integrity of being real. Not the last words in prayer perhaps, but understandable, truthful and, on the darkest days, quite relatable words.

The prayer is for help and wisdom in the face of existential threat.

Restrain yourself no longer, O God, the threat to our lives, our communities and our values is so overwhelming that we are beside ourselves with fear. We cannot bear the thought that our heritage will be lost and that our hopes for the future are in vain. Do not now restrain yourself! Reign in the forces of evil and threat, and give us the resolve to do what we can to live in ways that will make the future a time of fulfilment for generations yet to come.

There is real and desperate passion in this psalm; the feelings are unfiltered and the desire for assistance palpable. This is what makes the prayer live, but do we need the threat of extinction to draw us to true prayer?

---

100 NRSV.
101 Alter, p. 295.

Psalm 84: One day in thy courts

This is a beautiful poem of spiritual longing and fulfilment. It is often described as a pilgrim psalm, and it conveys a real sense of anticipation and hope of arrival. The psalm seems to fit on the road to Jerusalem. The pilgrims have stopped for the evening and, after a difficult day, sit together and recall the reason for the journey and the aesthetic and spiritual fulfilment of arrival at the temple in the past.

Psalm 84 is a celebration of Zion, one of several such 'Zion songs'.[102] But you don't need to have been to Jerusalem, or to have worked as a doorkeeper at the temple, to resonate with what it is saying about the profound joy of being in a holy place with good people and with having time to attend to matters of the spirit – worship, prayer, thanksgiving – and allowing a sense of the Lord of hosts to fill your heart and imagination.

Like all good pilgrimage, and all holy places, this psalm generates a sense not merely of human accomplishment and pleasure, but of God's presence. The three 'beatitudes' of the psalm show precisely this progression. In the first it is the one who dwells in God's house who is blessed. In the second the blessed one is the person whose strength is in God and who has internalized God's ways, and the final half-verse celebrates the one whose blessedness comprises their trust in God. The journey is from distance to presence, to learning, and to trust. Such is the journey of faith.

The prayer is that we may travel well and settle in a place of blessings.

Bless all our journeys, O Lord, with the joy of arriving at the place where your glory abides. When we drift away from your loving presence, guide us home. When we are in danger or difficulty, come to meet us. And when we find ourselves in a good place, teach us to delight in it and to desire nothing more than to stay and serve with humility and grace that we may receive the blessings that come to all who trust in you.

The sense of God's presence is clearly not something that can ever be guaranteed, but it does seem to be more associated with some places than others. Do these associations tell us more about God or about people?

---

102 The Zion songs are Psalms 46, 48, 76, 84, 87 and 122.

Psalm 85: Truth will flourish

This psalm is about restored fortunes, forgiveness and peace. Its tone is honest, reflective and positive. In the early verses, God is reminded of past acts of forgiveness, and these are imagined as the turning away of anger. Perceiving God's current indignation, the writer pleas for God to be forgiving, 'wilt thou not turn again and quicken us : that thy people may rejoice in thee?' The prayer is richly rewarded with the prophecy of peace. Salvation is 'nigh' and not only is there peace in the land but there is also glory.

Then we come to the most famous verses in the psalm, a justifiably renowned celebration of the values and realities that characterize ultimate reconciliation. First, 'Mercy and truth are met together : righteousness and peace have kissed each other.' And then anther pattern is suggested – truth comes from below, and righteousness (or justice) from above: 'Truth shall flourish out of the earth : and righteousness hath looked down from heaven.'

The psalm concludes by affirming that the land will be blessed and the people will live well, restored by the loving-kindness of God that, because it involves truth and justice as well as kindness and peace, is ultimately and beautifully reconciling.

The prayer is that God would direct us towards truth and justice.

O God, by whose loving-kindness and mercy we are forgiven and restored, teach us ever to seek the truth and to strive for justice, that your glory may dwell in our land and that we may know the peace of both personal calm and of a well ordered society.

This psalm suggests that justice, truth, mercy and peace are all integrally connected and vitally important. It might also invite us to reflect on the nature of these fundamental values and what they add to each other.

Psalm 86: Knit my heart unto thee

The power of this psalm is in the overall message that the needs that we present to God are more than met by God's power and inclination to help. It is carried along rhetorically by the intermingling of statements of our need with descriptions of God. Ultimately, petition is more than answered by description.

The psalm begins on a bad day, 'I am poor, and in misery.' It continues with many pleas for mercy, comfort, or even any kind of hearing. But when the writer dares to remember the worst of times it is positively, 'thou hast delivered my soul from the nethermost hell'.

Although there is an unusually strong emphasis on seeking mercy in this psalm there is nothing in it that is unfamiliar to the reader of the Psalter thus far. Many of the verses repeat words and sentiments of earlier psalms. What makes the psalm special is the overall force of putting these pithy statements together, and showing how God oversupplies for our needs. And among all the familiar phrases there is a unique and beautiful image of the desire for intimacy with God, 'O knit my heart unto thee, that I may fear thy name.' Although more recent scholarship understands this image as one of unity or integrity within the person, rather than of relationship with God, we can perhaps draw an insight from the error and see personal integrity and closeness to God as closely related aspirations.

The prayer is for saving reconciliation with ourselves and with God.

Keep us mindful, gracious God, of the love that brought us out of the trouble that we have caused for ourselves, and of the suffering that has been inflicted on us by others. Focus our minds on your patience, your goodness and your truth. Knit our hearts to your heart, that as we become as one with your love we may become more fully reconciled to ourselves.

Although this psalm is built on many familiar phrases it offers fresh insights and new wisdom. There is an invitation here to reflect on where we might best look for the wisdom to navigate the challenges that the future will bring.

Psalm 87: My fresh springs

This short psalm acclaims and celebrates Jerusalem, Sion,[103] as the abode of the God of all peoples. It is the city of God in the broadest, grandest and also most inclusive sense. Even those who are far from it are its spiritual inhabitants; they have their roots and origins in the place of God's presence.

The final verse suggests a context of procession and liturgy, reinforcing the note of celebration that is central to these few verses. The final words, 'All my fresh springs shall be in thee', would be sung by singers and dancers,[104] and suggest that Sion is the place not only of origins but also of renewal.

The prayer invites us to accept that our faith is God's ongoing gift in us.

Strengthen our faith, O God of all, with the recollection that its origins lie not in our own will or decision, but in your abiding presence and dynamic providence; and as we call to mind your eternal love, renew and refresh us with your ever-flowing spirit.

This is another psalm that invites us to reflect on where we might find the God-given 'newness', the spiritual freshness and inspiration, that will help us navigate the future.

---

103 The Prayer Book uses 'Sion', but the more familiar form today is 'Zion'. Both forms are used here depending only on which translation is being quoted or referenced.
104 The word 'trumpeters', which appears in the Prayer Book, is elsewhere translated 'dancers'.

Psalm 88: The lowest pit

This is a unique psalm not because it names sadness and expresses lament, but because this is *all* it does. Other lament psalms express the dark side of human experience but in the end the writer finds a candle in the gloom. This is not what happens in Psalm 88, however. It is a raw poem indeed; remarkable for its emotional honesty and vulnerability.

To read this psalm is to embark on a descent. Imagine the writer on a stone staircase that descends into a darkened pit. The staircase spirals around a central space. At first the words describe the experience of descending into gloom, but the descent gets worse as the writer comes to feel that what has happened isn't just unfortunate but is somehow in accord with God's design or intention, 'Thou hast laid me in the lowest pit : in a place of darkness, and in the deep.' Complaints and laments then blend together and make an unremitting cry of despair which is punctuated only by protest. This really is hopeless! What is to be gained? Why this fate? Why this alienation? 'Lord, why abhorest thou my soul : and hidest thou thy face from me?' All source of comfort is gone as it concludes, 'My lovers and friends hast thou put away from me : and hid mine acquaintance out of my sight.'

And there it ends. The light is completely extinguished.

The prayer comes from the depth of dark experience.

Accept, O God, the reality of my darkest times. The days when anxiety turns to despair and loneliness becomes paranoia. The days when I see no brightness in the sunlight, when there is no person I can call on as a friend. The days when I experience no love at all from my fellows. Accept as my prayer, O God, this description of my life, not because it is offered with faith and hope, but because, even in this awful alienation, I trust that you might hear, that you might heal, and that you might in time raise me from this deep and dark pit.

It takes real courage to bring our absolutely worst experiences into prayer, but might being truthful about the depth of our despair before God itself be to strike a flint that kindles a light?

Psalm 89: Thou hast broken the covenant

Psalm 89 brings to a conclusion the third of the five books of psalms. The last half-verse is therefore not a conclusion to this psalm itself but to the third book as a whole. The psalm actually ends at verse 50 with the words 'Wherewith thine enemies have blasphemed thee, and slandered the footsteps of thine Anointed.' It's clear, then, that the theme of the whole long psalm is deep disappointment and the questioning of faith and of God that follows from it.

Verses 1–36, however, are all positive: they praise God's power and celebrate God's promises. Steadfast love and faithfulness are the most appreciated of divine attributes, and they are repeatedly extolled. Certainly, there will be times when things go awry and God will then respond negatively, yet this all takes place within an overall context of loving-kindness and faithfulness.

But, or rather, 'BUT!', in verse 37 the tone changes radically. God has not lived up to these promises. God has let the people down. The spirituality of praise has been replaced by the spirituality of disappointment. And just as Psalm 88 did not allow the mood of darkening despair to be lightened, so this psalm does not take the edge off the experience of disappointment. Indeed, when we read verses 1–36 knowing where the writer is going to take us, even they have a bitter taste.

The prayer is one of talking back to God from the experience of disappointment.

O God, whose praise we have sung from our hearts, whose steadfast love is the bedrock of our life and whose faithfulness is the source of all our hope, look down, we pray, on the dissolution of our communities and the destruction of our institutions. The forces of chaos have destroyed our traditions and even our weather has lost its familiar patterns. Hear our confusion, feel our disappointment, and remember your promises, your power and the loving-kindness that we have so often praised.

The journey of the psalm taken as a whole is towards giving full expression to our disappointment with God. Its paradoxical and thought-provoking message is that even disappointment with God can be a form of faithfulness.

Psalm 90: A thousand years in thy sight

The reality of time shapes this psalm. First, God's unbounded time, which stretches back before the dawn of geology, 'Before the mountains were brought forth' and in which a thousand years are 'but as yesterday'. And second, the pulse of limited human time, the 'threescore years and ten', or perhaps 'fourscore', but 'so soon passeth it away, and we are gone'. The psalm, which is associated with Moses, also references a third type of time, 'crisis time'. The moment is difficult and worrying; vulnerability and fragility have become apparent. There is hope that the time of difficulty that the people are now encountering will soon come to an end. And there is prayer that the concern that directs this psalm, that our time is running out, will focus minds and hearts so that the people might address the situation wisely, 'So teach us to number our days : that we may apply our hearts unto wisdom.'

The psalm ends with a plea for collaboration. God's work is needed and invited but the people are working too. Their hands are busy trying to sort things out, and that effort is offered as the psalm concludes, 'O prosper thou our handy-work.'

The prayer seeks to give the same perspective to a current crisis.

O God of the endless ages, as we look to you from the midst of our current crisis, we are overwhelmed by our lack of power, our lack of wisdom and our lack of time. Look with pity on our condition, console our hearts, and strengthen our resolve. Bless all who seek your will, and all who are working to further your purposes.

To move in one poem from unimaginable eons of geological time to the desperate crisis of the current moment is to expect a great deal of our imagination. And yet this imaginative dexterity is precisely what we lack when we panic about time.

Psalm 91: Thou art my hope

The theme of God's protection of those who seek it is strong in this psalm. Consider the verbs: God delivers, covers, protects, answers, accompanies and rescues. It is a psalm that strongly encourages trust. The very last word of the last verse is 'salvation', and this is the trajectory of the whole poem. Dangers are noted, causes for fear enumerated, and the perils associated with different times of day are spelt out. There is trouble all around. This is understood not as personal danger but as punishment for the wicked and the ungodly. The message is simple, 'trust God, prayerfully put yourself under God's protection, and you will find that although you are surrounded by horrors of all kinds you are a spectator not a participant'. The trouble is definitely real but there is an encouraging promise, 'it shall not come nigh thee'.

As in the previous psalm, God is a refuge: a hope and a 'strong hold'. This is a psalm to settle the nerves, and since the time of St Benedict has been one that monastics would know by heart and recite in the darkness of their chapel at the final service of the day, Compline. Given the number of images and ideas in this psalm that could provoke nightmares, this could be a seen to be an imprudent choice. However, the spirituality here is not the Zen practice of clearing the mind, but the Judeo-Christian wisdom of naming demons and facing fears. The thought is not, as in some psalms, 'let me flee all this'. Rather it is something like, 'bring it on! I will live boldly through the cycles of daily time, whatever psychological or material troubles they might bring. For I trust in God 24/7.'

The prayer is one for realism trust and protection.

Give us the wisdom, O God, to name our deepest fears and most troubling anxieties; embolden us to trust thee with the concerns that beset us by night and by day, and lead us through the years, trusting in thy protection whatever troubles surround us.

The extent to which the psalms use vivid and emotive language and imagery is obvious and evident, but contrasting it with a Buddhist approach raises many questions about what we mean by 'spirituality'.

Psalm 92: How glorious are thy works

This joyful psalm is full of confidence and redolent with images that speak of the strength that belongs to the faithful. Uniquely the superscription assigns it to the Sabbath day, and the themes fit with that weekly reminder that it is God who orders not only creation but also political and civic life. The poet is not questioning their own righteousness; this is the song of a faithful person in which personal enemies are also God's enemies. This poet is confident that they have chosen the way of God, and the way of wisdom – and equally confident that many others have chosen a different way.

Evildoers indeed make their havoc, but verses 7–11 declare that God puts things right. A sense of order and the prevailing power of goodness lie behind the delight in singing and praising with which the psalm begins. The affirmation that it is good to give thanks, to sing praises around the clock, opens out into the idea that such praising isn't a matter of inner spiritual song or a personal solo only, but that it calls for instrumental music too.

The psalm ends with a double celebration: both the settled strength of the faithful likened, in an image that reminds us of Psalm 1, to well-rooted and flourishing trees and the righteousness and power of the Lord.

The prayer is that we might live faithfully.

We give thee thanks, O thou Most High, for the gifts of faith and of gladness. Keep us, we pray, active in prayer, fervent in praise, joyful in speech, prudent in action and secure in thy righteousness.

This Sabbath poem invites us to reflect on whether we are adequately disciplined in setting time aside for things of the spirit, for our relationship with God and for rest and recuperation.

Psalm 93: The floods are risen

This is the first of a series of psalms that expand on the idea that the Lord is King. Psalms 93–100 constitute a cluster of psalms that are central to the whole book, and which has been called 'the theological heart of the Psalter'.[105] Psalm 94 is something of an outlier here, but the others are full of confidence, joy and energy, the general theme being that 'the Lord is King and it is time to sing a new song'. This is a very different world from the psalms that are laden with lament and complaint that we have encountered earlier; that contrast being one of the justifications for feeling that while it might be an overstatement to say that 'the whole of life is here' it is clear that the Psalter covers a vast range of emotional territory.

Psalm 93 is a short celebration of the power of the king over the forces of evil and chaos. The proclamation is first that the creation is absolutely solid and intact, and this is followed by the assertion that whatever rises up to threaten the good order of things with chaos and anarchy – the sea being imagined as the place of chaos once again – is a lesser power than the transcendent and all-powerful God. It is this that justifies the evocative final words, 'holiness becometh thine house for ever' – an indirect invitation to the reader to adopt an attitude of peaceful, unhurried, un-anxious calm.

The prayer is for personal peace and confidence.

Give us, O Lord, the faith that makes us peaceful: peaceful in our hearts and peaceful in our relationships with others. Fill us with wonder when we consider the expanses of space and time that have flowed from your creative love, and give us confidence in your goodness when we see the forces of chaos and hostility gathering their energies. Bless us, O Lord, with the peace that comes from faith and trust, that we may know your holiness and reflect your glory.

The sea is used in the psalms to represent the chaos that threatens divine order, but in an increasingly urbanized world that imagery may no longer be as powerful as it was. Are there more convincing images of chaos today?

---

105 J. C. McCann Jr., quoted by Brueggemann and Bellinger, p. 402.

Psalm 94: Thy mercy held me up

In this psalm, the prayer of those who long for justice is presented to God as the trustworthy judge of the world. It is a psalm of powerful emotions, in particular fear, coupled with indignation at the arrogance and insouciance of the wicked. These are the feelings that lie behind the appeal to God's vengeance in the first verse. Quite what is meant by the word rendered 'vengeance' here is disputed. Some see it as a cool appeal to dispassionate punishment, or 'retribution' and use that sort of register in translation, but Alter is convinced that the word 'vengeance' is correct in its more hot-blooded sense, describing it as 'a boldly aggressive characterization of God'.[106]

The psalm goes through several different moods. The opening verses are of lament and complaint. It then modulates into a more patronizing style with rhetorical questions and the sorts of points that those who suffer often have to put up with from their would-be comforters. The final section shows the writer as having moved on from question and instruction to a more settled faithfulness, based, it would seem, not only on faith in God's power but also on the understanding that, despite the roughness of our sentiments, God does actually listen. Verse 17 in the Prayer Book version isn't especially clear, but it is plainer in a more recent translation: 'If the Lord had not been my help, my soul would soon have lived in the land of silence.'[107]

This psalm is not only about being helped by God but also about being heard by God. It hints that there is a virtuous circle here: that it is being helped by God that keeps us speaking and thinking. In other words, God helps us both to get away from trouble and to embark upon intelligent and thoughtful action as responsible agents.

The prayer is for those who are affronted by injustice.

O God to whom justice belongs, show yourself in the affairs of this world and bring to account those who flout your commandments and pay no heed to the wellbeing of others. Be with all who seek to walk with integrity, who try to deal compassionately with their neighbours, and who long for fairness. Arise, O judge of the earth, and make yourself known, that justice may triumph in our homes and our communities.

The harmful actions of others rightly prompt emotional responses. But what follows? If we ignore our emotions, we soon lack integrity and energy. If we follow them uncritically, we can slip into the vicious vortex of vengeance.

---

106 Alter, p. 331
107 NRSV

Psalm 95: A great God

This is a psalm of two halves. The first is a joyful call to worship, poetically and forcefully written. The theology, however, is a little ambiguous. On the one hand God is the maker of everything including human beings, on the other hand there is a strong hint that this psalm embraces some form of polytheism since God is 'a great King above all gods'. This could be a pre-monotheistic echo, but it might be just a poetically helpful turn of phrase. In any case, the God whom we are being invited to worship is the premier, the creator, the one who has a covenant with his people. God makes all, God makes us, and God cares for us – that is the basis of worship as understood here.

Then the psalm changes its tune. Now it is God's turn to speak, and we can detect at least some tired exasperation in the tone. 'To-day, if ye will hear his voice, harden not your hearts' meaning, 'O that today you would listen to his voice'[108] or 'If you would only hear his voice!'[109] The psalm goes on to reveal that the historical record of God's chosen people is not good. Liberated from Egypt they quickly became discontented in the wilderness and decided that they would test God. God was grieved and angered and determined that they should not enter the Promised Land.

The message is clear. Worship is wonderful but worship without faith and action leads only as far as the wilderness. 'Rest', the last word of the psalm, comes not to those who grumble and complain, but to those who are faithful in worship and in action.

The prayer is that we might worship well.

Accept our praise and thanksgiving, O God, creator and redeemer of all, and inspire us to open our hearts to receive the blessing of your love, that we may worship you through our words, our actions and our attitudes, and that in the fullness of time we may know the joy of your peace.

Reflecting on this psalm we might either ponder the nature of our spiritual desires and hopes, or think about the ethics and attitudes that God requires of us – or perhaps think yet more about how they connect.

---

108 NRSV.
109 Alter, p. 337.

Psalm 96: The beauty of holiness

Two themes are important in this assertive poem. The first is the imperative to sing to the Lord a new song.[110] In the case of Psalm 96 there is a little irony here, as much of the wording that follows is familiar and some is almost verbatim quotation from elsewhere in the Psalter; at least one scholar has described psalm as a 'mosaic'.[111] The newness being invoked here is not therefore 'novelty' exactly; it's more like 'freshness'.

The other theme is that this appeal to sing to God is not addressed just to those who are nearby, nor only to God's people, but to 'all the whole earth'. This is a psalm of great theological vision and grand ambition. It's as if the whole of everything is invited to resonate responsively to its true sovereign, its only king. And perhaps this is what 'the beauty of holiness' means. However, this is not a psalm predicated primarily on aesthetics or even on the grandeur of creation. The final verse makes it clear that, wonderful as all that is in the present moment, of even greater significance is the belief that in the future God will come and judge with righteousness and truth. It's when we believe this that we can praise the one God who is creator of all because the same and only God is also the champion of justice.

In verse 10 there is the bold invitation to proclaim that 'The Lord is King'. This is in contrast to 'all the gods of the heathen' mentioned in verse 5. The echoes of polytheism are not to be taken at face value here. The message is that there is something singular and transcendent about Israel's God, Yahweh, and something very inferior about the gods of other people. They are classed as 'idols' or, as Alter more literally translates, 'ungods'.[112]

Christians have often associated it with Christmas and Epiphany, reading it as an imperative to tell good news to the whole earth.[113]

The prayer is that we may join in worthily with creation's praise.

O God, the creator, king and judge of all, bless us with such a profound sense of your love and your justice that we may always find new ways to sing your praise and to rejoice in the beauty of true holiness.

Many who love the psalms will warm to the phrase, 'the beauty of holiness', but find it difficult to be precise about its meaning. Might it be that this very lack of precision is an important part of what the word 'beauty' adds to 'holiness'?

---

110 Psalm 98 starts with the same words.
111 The point is made by Yair Hoffman, cited by Alter, p. 338.
112 Alter, p. 339.
113 See Brueggemann and Bellinger, p. 417.

Psalm 97: Rejoice in the Lord

This psalm is similar to the previous one in its emphasis on the unrivalled sovereignty of God. Its imagery is somewhat different, however, there being no mention of the subduing of the sea. Instead we have the rather violent pictures of thunderbolt-throwing and mountain-melting. Also, while it was the gods who were exposed as idols in Psalm 96, it is the worshippers of idols who are the focus of derisory attention here: 'Confounded be all they that worship carved images, and delight in vain gods.'

Quite where all this violent imagery comes from is uncertain and some suggest that it is adopted from other traditions rather than being intrinsic to Yahweh-worship. It is clear, however, that while the images are terrifying, the total context is positive. The psalm begins and ends with the invitation to 'be glad' or 'rejoice'.[114]

Another troubling use of language in the psalm is the encouragement to hate, though if anything is hate-worthy it is surely, 'the thing which is evil'. The notion of hate is a dangerous one, however, as is the imagery of divine destructiveness. This is a psalm that pushes the boundaries that limit how we might describe and respond to the sovereignty of God. But that is not a criticism. It is rather a description of what the psalms, at their best, both do and encourage.

The prayer is that we might trust in God's might and universal goodwill.

Teach us so to rejoice in thy sovereign majesty, O God, that we may always trust in your power to save, and never resort to violence in your name or stoop to hate those whom we oppose. Strengthen us in faith, ground us in hope and unite us in the joy and gladness that reflects your benevolent intentions for us and for all creation.

Like many psalms, this one invites us to extend the range of our prayer-life. It invites us to ask ourselves whether we have any unnecessary constrictions in our praying.

---

114 Coverdale uses the words 'glad' in verse 1 and 'rejoice' in the final verse, but most translations use 'rejoice' at the beginning and the end.

Psalm 98: Show yourselves joyful

Similar to Psalm 96 in several ways, Psalm 98 exemplifies one of the typical shapes of the psalms of praise: first the community is enjoined to praise the Lord, then it is given reasons for doing so. Rehearsing the reasons for praise is itself, of course, one of the ways to praise God, and so recitation of the psalm, if done with integrity, immediately achieves the purpose of the psalm. But such integrity is a matter of style as well as of substance. 'Show yourselves joyful unto the Lord, all ye lands : sing, rejoice, and give thanks.' There is more than a hint here that the emotions must be in tune with the words. 'Make a joyful noise' reads one contemporary translation, 'break forth into joyous song and sing praises.'[115] Exuberance and enthusiasm are being looked for here, a sense that there is powerful energy within that seeks release in this most positive of forms.

The invitation is cast widely; not only to God's people but also to the sea which is to 'make a noise' or 'roar' and the floods (or rivers) which are asked to 'clap their hands'. The hills and mountains are to join in too. There is a similar sentiment in Psalm 96, but there is more exuberance in Psalm 98, perhaps because the memory of liberation packs a more powerful punch than does a sense of having been created. In both cases, however, the rejoicing is in the context of taking to heart the promise of justice.

The prayer is that we together with all creation might rejoice in God.

Make our hearts glad, O Lord God, as we sing thy praise in psalms and hymns and spiritual songs, and let us show ourselves joyful in witness to thy great love and abiding mercy. O maker of all, inspire the whole creation to respond with the sound of thanksgiving, for thou art a God of justice and of truth, and thou art God alone.

The connection being made in this psalm between sounds of various kinds and joyfulness is an intriguing counterpoint to the emphasis on silence and stillness found in some other psalms. Maybe there is a time and place for both.

---

115 NRSV.

Psalm 99: Fall down before his footstool

This psalm is about God's reign. In fact, the first line is better translated not as 'The Lord is King' but 'The Lord reigns.'[116] The difference is between noun and verb, between being and doing – and the original is in favour of doing. So this isn't about status, but about the kind of activity in which God engages. This matters because the actual theme of the psalm is holiness. That God is holy is the reason to magnify or exalt or extol God. But while holiness is often understood as distance, a crude interpretation of what it means to be 'set aside', holiness here is about connectedness, relationality and responsiveness.

God is not a super-posh-toff, not the ultimate aristocrat in whose lofty presence we should tremble because we are so inferior. No, God's holiness makes us tremble precisely because God does care, engage and relate – and all in the pursuit of fairness and justice. Priests and prophets call out to God, and God hears. Moreover, God answers. And this same God gives a careful response, forgiving on some occasions and punishing when appropriate.

If this is 'set-apartness' it is not aloofness but commitment and loyalty to a people whose commitment and loyalty is expected in return. This is holiness as faithfulness. The point here is not so much that God is good in the abstract; more that God is good to know. That understanding runs through this psalm and is the reason for the worship on God's home turf – God's own 'holy hill'.

The prayer is for daily holiness.

O holy God, make us holy as you are holy. Holy with passion for justice, holy with unending love, holy in finding apt words, and holy in our praise of your great goodness and undying loyalty.

The ways in which we think about God are always inadequate, but some ways are far more misleading than others. That God loves us deeply and yet also inspires in us a feeling of awe so that we tremble at the presence of the Lord is a paradox to ponder.

---

116 Alter, p. 328.

Psalm 100: Be joyful

Psalm 100 is the most refined distillation of joy and gladness in God in the Psalter, if not in the whole Bible. Brief and direct, it is full of imperatives. We are to be joyful, to worship, to know, to enter gates and to give thanks and to bless God – or 'speak good of his Name'. But this isn't mere instruction. Reasons are given too: it is primarily because 'The Lord', that is Yahweh – the creator, liberator and carer – really is God, 'Be ye sure that the Lord he is God : it is he that hath made us, and not we ourselves.'

Behind the joyful praising there is theological discovery or conviction. In a word, there is 'faith'. It is the faith that the Lord is good for us and good for our children and good for their children.

This simple psalm of joy is rooted in the goodness of God, but notice one apparently small detail in the wording. It's not just the faithful who are invited to be joyful; it is 'all ye lands'. The good news here is for all people and all creation. That is why the joy is so profound and compelling.

The prayer is that we might be joyful in our daily living.

Make us joyful, O God: joyful in faith, joyful in hope and joyful in love; that together with all creation we may give thanks for you grace, your mercy and your truth.

This simple hymn of joy might help us to remember that joy is an important part of life, and encourage us to relax and appreciate the more joyful aspects of everyday life.

Psalm 101: The way of godliness

Understood by many scholars to be among the royal psalms, this is fundamentally a psalm about the desire for wise living shaped by good values. While the virtues and attitudes that are enumerated here would always be fitting in a leader, they are not out of place in any member of the community. So the psalm can be said by anyone who hopes to be formed into the kind of character that is briefly described here. Such a character is defined by 'mercy and judgement', at the opening, a fine point of balance on which to begin.

The psalm presents wisdom that is not ideological, but which reflects the sort of God who is being revealed: one with the highest standards of fairness and yet also a deep commitment to personal love and care. Such values could corrupt good order when taken together, and that is why the actual values expressed here are so important. There is no space for malicious plotting, or perverseness, or slander. Haughtiness, magnificently envisaged as 'a proud look and high stomach', is also ruled out. Nor is there room for deceit or lying. Faithfulness and an inclination to honesty and straightforwardness are core values here.

The prayer is that our lives might reflect God's values and purposes.

Bless us O God, with the wisdom to seek to live our lives according to the values we learn from your holy word: encourage in us a deep loyalty for our friends, inspire us to seek justice for strangers. Make us passionate for truth and straightforward in speech and action, that with humility we might reflect your purposes in all that we do.

This psalm might prompt us to ask ourselves what qualities of character we hope to find in people of faith, and the extent to which we ourselves display them.

Psalm 102: I have eaten ashes

The three parts of this psalm might suggest to us that prayer is an ongoing process involving first the honest appraisal of our condition, second the remembrance of the nature and promises of God, and third the blending of real experience with the content of our faith. Certainly, the reality expressed in the first part (verses 1–11) is difficult. We might imagine the speaker here to have a terminal disease and to be riven with anxiety and physical discomfort. The middle section (verses 12–23) is less personal and certainly less desperate, being about both God and the wider social and civic context. The needs of the individual seem to be lost, as God's action is concerned with the salvation and restoration of the holy city, the historical context probably being the aftermath of the destruction of Jerusalem in the sixth century.

But personal suffering is not here eclipsed by the greater significance of major political movements. The point is that God cares about all levels of reality. Verse 25, for example, answers personal concern expressed in verse 24 with the remembrance: 'Thou, Lord, in the beginning hast laid the foundation of the earth : and the heavens are the work of thy hands.' Extending the horizon of concern beyond our own life, particularly to the future flourishing and faithfulness of the generations yet to come, ultimately both affirms our personal suffering and puts it in its place.

The prayer is for those who know their own frailty and fear the advance of death.

Hear our prayers, O God, for all who cry out to you from a place of despair, all whose bodies are failing and all whose lives are coming to an end in pain or distress. Bring them calm, bring them comfort, and bring them hope. Draw to their mind's eye the remembrance of good days, and thoughts of a future where their life's work will be appreciated and their children's children flourish and prosper.

The focus on frailty here might encourage us to reflect on the impact that the suffering of others makes on us, not least when it is our own turn to suffer.

Psalm 103: Mercy and loving-kindness

This psalm praises the steadfast love of God and emphasizes virtues and attributes that come to the fore in the teaching of Jesus and Paul: God's compassion, kindness and enduring love. It is personal and intimate, perhaps being the work of someone who is in dire need of the healing and forgiveness mentioned in verse 3. But it ends in a triumphant chorus of praise – the last three verses balancing the first three. Like Psalm 104, but also most unusually, the opening words are self-directed, in particular they are directed to the inner self, translated as 'soul'. 'Praise the Lord, O my soul : and all that is within me praise his holy name'.

However, the strong emphasis on mercy and forgiveness, and the kindly forbearance of God, should not be thought of as the only note in the psalm. The poet remembers that, 'The Lord executeth righteousness and judgement' and the law given to Moses is recalled in verse 7. The following verse is a direct quote from Exodus (34.6) but it omits reference to the notion of God's 'reckoning the crimes of the fathers' to the children's children.[117]

It is the forgiveness of God that gets the greatest emphasis here – and it is forgiveness not as a response to repentance, exactly, but as a reward for an appropriate and loyal regard for God, 'the Lord is merciful unto them that fear him'. God, envisaged as a father in relation to his own children, recognizes the frailty of the flesh and the limits of mortals. This passage is familiar from its use at the graveside, and culminates in these deeply consoling words, 'But the merciful goodness of the Lord endureth for ever and ever upon them that fear him ...'.

The prayer is that we may know God's love.

Touch our hearts, O God, with the knowledge of thy love, fill our souls with the assurance of thy forgiveness that we may be healed, renewed and restored to fullness of life and come to take our place in the glad company of all who praise thee and please thee.

Recognizing that both forgiveness and healing are important, we might reflect on how they relate to each other.

---

117 Alter makes this point, p. 359.

Psalm 104: The earth shall tremble

This psalm is a celebration of God's work in and through creation, and meditates ecstatically on the beauty and glory of the natural world. It is worth noting in our scientific culture today that there is no attempt to explain anything in this response to creation.

There is a great deal of poetic description in which God is seen as active and present and engaged in this astonishingly beautiful and generative world. The creation is itself creative, and this is understood as the ongoing activity of the creator. There is a strong sense of the interconnectedness of things and of the providential organization of the ecosystem. There is no rivalry with the scientific 'how' of the natural world as the focus is on the 'thatness' of creation. The natural world doesn't prompt curiosity, 'where did all this come from and why it is as it is?' Rather it arouses wonder: 'this world is marvellous, how awesome must the creator be!' And so it begins and ends with invitations, including to the self, to bless and thank.

The tone is calm. The sense of order is profound. Even the usually terrifying Leviathan or dragon-like sea monster is not seen as a threat but is observed at play: 'There go the ships, and there is that Leviathan : whom thou hast made to take his pastime therein.' We are invited to imagine whales larking around in the deep. But while creation is wonderful, it is the creator who has the capacity to frighten, 'The earth shall tremble at the look of him : if he do but touch the hills, they shall smoke.'

This great psalm invites us to wonder at the glory of the world as well as the glory of God, and encourages us to voice our praise and thanksgiving to the Lord of all.

The prayer is that we should be good stewards of creation.

O Holy Spirit of God, who brooded over the waters at the dawn of time, and whose breath brings life to the world and joy to the heart of humankind, give us such a profound sense of gratitude for all the blessings of life that we never cease to sing your praise, nor to delight in the diversity of creation, nor to accept responsibility for the stewardship of this world; that we might live joyfully and well, and pass on all that we have inherited to the generations yet to come.

The emphasis on the natural world in this psalm prompts us to reflect on our attitudes towards the environment. In particular, we might ponder the balance of curiosity and wonder in our mind-set and spirituality.

Psalm 105: All his wondrous works

Rather like the even longer Psalm 78, this one offers a summary of the important episodes of the early history of the people of Israel in verse. This has led scholars to conclude that it was recited on important ritual occasions in the temple. The psalm takes the community gathered for its recitation on a journey from God's promise to Abraham, Isaac and Jacob to the story of Joseph in Egypt, to the enslavement of the Hebrew people and their liberation (after vividly described plagues) and their subsequent sojourn in the wilderness, until at last it comes to the entry into the Promised Land. That such a story is reassuring is beyond doubt. It is also a source of genuine wonder, though in a different way to Psalm 104 which was a response to the natural world.

But the story is also troubling in its political overtones, made quite explicit in the penultimate verse, 'And [The Lord God] gave them the lands of the heathen : and they took the labours of the people in possession.' Our reading of it, and our spiritual response, need not be dominated by the politics of land grab, however. It's the hand of God in history that matters most, together with the attitude of 'abiding astonishment', a phase that the twentieth century Jewish sage Martin Buber coined to summarize the human response to such action.[118]

The conclusion to which this whole recitation is driving, and which is expressed in the final verse. '[All this took place so] 'That they might keep his statutes : and observe his laws.' That is, this all happened to create the conditions for loyal obedience to torah – to give God's people the opportunity to follow the principles that were delivered to their ancestors on the journey described, and become people who walk in the transformative way of the Lord.

The prayer is that we celebrate our privileges and remember our history responsibly.

Bless us, O God, with abiding astonishment when we appreciate the privileges and opportunities that we enjoy today, and help us to recognize our indebtedness to the guiding hand of your providence. Inspire us to seek your face in the present moment as well as in the events of the past, and encourage us to follow your guidance, that the future may be a time of blessing and justice for all.

Buber's phrase 'abiding astonishment' is a powerful one. To what extent does it connect with your experience, or speak to your sense of God?

---

118 Brueggemann and Bellinger mention this, p. 452.

Psalm 106: Noble acts of the Lord

Psalm 106 brings to a conclusion the Fourth Book of Psalms, which was probably composed during the exile and which often looks back historically for encouragement. 'God got us out of trouble before and will do so again' has been a recurring theme. It is a surprising psalm in as much as it begins as if it is going to be a fulsome song of praise, but after a few verses it quickly turns to an extended recollection of the faults of the ancestors. God has been faithful to the covenant, but the people were not very faithful at all.

Some very familiar events are narrated here, but whereas Psalm 105 draws attention to God's faithfulness and power, Psalm 106 shines the spotlight on the community's failure to respond well. There are several incidences of this as the 46-verse long psalm depicts the ebb and flow of faithfulness and sin. For instance, the response to being liberated from slavery in Egypt is initially good, 'Then they believed his words : and sang praise unto him', but soon it went wrong. 'But within a while they forgat his works : and would not abide his counsel. But lust came upon them in the wilderness : and they tempted God in the desert.'

Confession of faults in faith is the main theme of this psalm, and so the penultimate verse is the natural conclusion: 'Deliver us, O Lord our God, and gather us from among the heathen : that we may give our thanks to thy holy Name, and make our boast of thy praise.' One wonders whether God would be convinced by the promise, but the point is that God is faithful whether or not the people keep their promises. The doxology that concludes the Fourth Book of Psalms takes the form of a benediction.

The prayer blends confession of failure with petition for help.

Hear our prayer, O God, for we recognize our failure to be faithful and trusting, and confess our negligence of thankfulness and praise. Protect us against the worldly forces that threaten our peace and any powers that may harm us, and bring us all to a mature faith and to an abiding love of your way.

The faults of our ancestors can excite much emotion today. Maybe the question of what people will think of our own ethical practices and spiritual assumptions in 50 years time is also worthy of consideration.

Psalm 107: Declare the wonders

This long psalm is a collective prayer of thanksgiving to God. Unlike some psalms of praise, which can be a little abstract or generic, this one is quite specific, identifying four particular groups of people who are helped or rescued by God and who, as a result, offer their thanks. This detailed descriptive writing, which is full of imagery and drama, is framed by the opening verses, 'Let them give thanks whom the Lord hath redeemed : and delivered from the hand of the enemy.' The four specific examples are those lost in the desert, those in prison, the sick and those caught in a storm at sea.

As we read through these dramas we see the different circumstances depicted in some detail, but the style of the poetry makes us appreciate that whatever the circumstances, 'cries are cries', 'trouble is trouble' and 'deliverance is deliverance' and that, when we respond, 'thanksgiving is thanksgiving'. The point is not that God has a particular concern for these specific situations; God does not prefer those in peril on the sea to those who are endangered in the mountains. God's concern is for actual people, whatever their trouble. If prepared to think poetically, the landlocked can say a psalm about God rescuing them from a storm at sea, even though their own trouble with water is likely to be flood or drought or pollution. But the real message and power of Psalm 107 is in the final verse 'Whoso is wise will ponder these things : and they shall understand the loving-kindness of the Lord.' It is a direct and personal invitation to meditate on actual realties.

The prayer is of thanksgiving for deliverance from danger.

We join our own prayers of thanks, O God, with the thanksgivings of all people who have been delivered from danger. Help us to recall with gratitude the occasions when we (and those whom we love) have been close to death, and bring us to an ever-keener appreciation of your constant care and practical loving-kindness towards us.

Taken as a whole, Psalm 107 is an invitation to think of all our difficulties and dangers against the background of God's love. It can prompt us to reflect on how we have experienced danger and interpreted escape and rescue in the past.

Psalm 108: Awake, thou lute, and harp

Psalm 108 draws together verses from Psalms 57 and 60 to make a new poem. The first part is full of the urgent desire to express thanks and praise: 'O God, my heart is ready, my heart is ready.' The word 'ready' is often translated 'firm' or 'steadfast', but the idea that there is urgency and energy here is borne out with the desire to 'awake right early', rendered by more recent translators as the even more vivid 'I will awake the dawn.'[119] The sense of the power of God's benevolent qualities is also strong. God's mercy is 'greater than the heavens' and God's truth 'reacheth unto the clouds'.

The quotation from Psalm 60 remains positive, but the shadow of threat is palpable. In particular, there is a need for the beloved to be delivered, and God is petitioned for help, and then reminded of former promises and achievements. This leads on to renewed and even more urgent petition, and a note of desperation is heard, 'Hast thou not forsaken us, O God.' The hope is that this is very much not the case. The poet reminds the reader that human capacity is limited indeed and that it is God's help that is needed, 'for vain is the help of man'.

The final verse is confident that the prayer will be answered and that not only will there be deliverance but also achievement, 'Through God we shall do great acts.'

The prayer connects our own sense of spiritual drive with God's power and purposes.

Find within us, O God, the resolve to live with integrity, and touch our eyes with such a vision of your presence that we may glimpse your glory beyond all that we can see and within all that we encounter. Fix our hearts on your purposes, that we might awaken the dawn with your praise, acclaim your love near and far, and use all that we have been given by your grace to do great things.

The various translations of the state of the psalmist's heart in verse 1 invite us to reflect on the state of our own heart before God – whether it is 'ready', 'firm' or 'steadfast', or whether some other word would be more apt for us.

---

119 NRSV.

Psalm 109: I am helpless

This psalm is the prayer of a person who has been wronged in more than one way by someone who was once loved and trusted. 'They have spoken against me with false tongues : they compassed me about also with words of hatred, and fought against me without a cause.' The speaker has been good to this person, but all they have received in return is 'evil' and 'hatred'. That the psalmist is enraged about this betrayal is evident from what follows: 14 verses in which the desire for vengeance is spelt out in vivid detail. 'Let his days be few'; 'Let his children be fatherless'; 'Let his children be vagabonds'. The writer is on a roll, 'Let there be no man to pity him : nor to have compassion upon his fatherless children.'

Christian commentators struggle with all this, and it is easy to sympathize with those who mark up these verses to indicate that they are not appropriate for recitation in public worship. The issue to be addressed is this: does articulating this sort of thought aggravate feelings and incite others to follow the avenging example and lead on to hate-filled and unjust actions? Or, does it clear the air and pave the way for reconciliation and peace? This psalm is taken to support the latter view because it ends not with these bilious words but moves forward from them and ultimately concludes with prayers for personal protection and thanks to God. This is certainly not a psalm to set to a jolly tune for children to sing. But the invitation here is to own our most negative emotions and ventilate them in the presence of God, so that we might then adopt before others a more pacific response that focuses not on the need for vengeance, but on the need for impartial justice. It might be a dangerous thought, but there could sometimes be truth in it. For what else are we to do with our vengeful anger?

The prayer is for those who have suffered at the hands of those who have abused a position of trust.

Hear our anger, O God, and take up your cause against those who have abused their power to exploit the vulnerable in their care. Feel our rage, accept our indignation, and transform our passion for vengeance into a desire for justice. May those who have inflicted great harm come to understand what they have done, and those who have been deeply hurt find the healing they need and be restored to fullness of life and dignity.

The connection between the violently expressed feelings in the psalm and the abuse of power and exploitation of the vulnerable invites us to ask what other behaviours cause such a strong reaction in us, and whether they might be reflected in prayer.

Psalm 110: A priest for ever

This short, somewhat enigmatic, royal psalm is quoted no fewer than five times in the New Testament in support of the argument that Jesus is the Messiah. This is a theological reading, taking it to be a prophetic text, rather than an historical one, which would connect it with the kingship of David. It contains two divine oracles. The first is a declaration of the importance of the king and the second affirms the kings as a 'priest for ever after the order of Melchisedech'. Melchisedech is mentioned in Genesis 14 as the King of Salem who blessed Abram.

The first oracle is about the dignity, status and power of the king; kingly power also being the focus of the verses that immediately follow. The second oracle is concerned with holiness and righteousness, but also with power. The final verse has the king 'drink of the brook in the way'. Some see this as a reference to an aspect of the coronation ritual, some see it as prefiguring Christian baptism and some might see it as a more open reflection of the desire and need for refreshment that is more than material; remembering, perhaps, verse 1 of Psalm 42, 'Like as the hart desireth the water-brooks' or the 'waters of comfort' in Psalm 23. Certainly, the drinking is restorative of strength and confidence: 'therefore shall he lift up his head'.

The prayer is that those in positions of civic and political leadership might be supported and sustained.

Bless, O God, all those in positions of power and leadership with a profound sense of calling and the desire to seek the good of all; furnish them with wise advisers and careful counsellors, and guide them to places of refreshment, that they may lead others with the calm confidence that comes from steadfast faith in your love.

Some national leaders will lead from faith and commitment to serve, but others have different motives. This prompts an interesting question, 'does our responsibility to support a leader override any concern we might have about their motivation?'

Psalm 111: The beginning of wisdom

This is a classic 'psalm of praise' written as an acrostic in which the mighty acts of God are acclaimed. It begins 'Hallelujah' or 'Praise the Lord' though the Prayer Book version skips this and begins 'I will give thanks unto the Lord with my whole heart' which, according to distinctions made by some commentators, inaccurately moves the emphasis to thanksgiving from praise. The difference being that in praise we celebrate God's nature and attributes, whereas in thanksgiving we express gratitude for particular acts.

In this case the Lord is praised for his acts, which excuses the Prayer Book translation and suggests that the distinction between praise and thanksgiving is not always entirely straightforward or clear. Indeed, a theological response might be that in God 'doing' and 'being' are so integrally connected, so indivisible, that ultimately the praising/thanking distinction breaks down. This psalm certainly makes it plain that God is known through God's acts – though in typical Hebrew fashion the name of the Lord also matters. The Prayer Book has it as 'holy and reverend', while some recent translations have it is 'Holy and awesome'.[120]

The psalm ends with a comment not on God's praiseworthy nature or activities but on human wisdom, which begins with 'the fear of the Lord'. The NRSV translation of the end of this Psalm is clearer and more helpful than Coverdale's, 'The fear of the Lord is the beginning of wisdom; /all those who practise it have good understanding. / His praise endures for ever.'

The prayer in our thoughts and actions might reflect God's power and purpose.

Holy God, whose magnificent deeds inspire us to praise and yet cause us to tremble, calm our minds with the knowledge of your eternal benevolence, that your greatness might be our inspiration and that our words and works might bear witness to your endless love.

That the being/doing distinction breaks down when it comes to God raises the question of whether there are times when it breaks down for human beings too. Are there times when our actions and our essence are absolutely at one?

---

120 NRSV and Alter, p. 400, have the same wording.

Psalm 112: A good man

This psalm begins where Psalm 111 left off, with the virtue of fearing the Lord. It, too, is an acrostic, though a shorter one, with a new letter of the alphabet for each half verse. Whereas Psalm 111 celebrated the mighty acts of God, this one has its attention firmly fixed on the attributes and actions of a virtuous person. It is often described as a wisdom psalm, and similarly instructive material is found in other wisdom literature in the Bible. It is also similar to Psalm 1 in that both are extended beatitudes, so that some believe that this may be a restatement of that psalm in the very different historical context of the exile.[121]

The psalm is a reminder of blessedness to those who are in an alien country and culture and who have lost all the normal comforts and consolations of home. But what is this 'blessedness'? Not happiness or contentment or joyful gladness. The psalm is more to do with the rewards that come from the practice of virtues, the pursuit of righteousness under God and the particular pleasures that come from living a life of integrity, rather than one of dissipation or the pursuit of vain goals – in a word, sinfulness. The thought here, and it is made plain in the final verse, is that 'the desire of the ungodly shall perish'. That is, sin can make you very unhappy. But that doesn't quite mean that virtue and goodness make you happy, as happiness is commonly understood. The language and thought of the psalm is much richer than the concept of happiness. It points to a way of living in which the good life makes good sense under the ultimate reign of a good God; even when times are hard. It is a psalm that invites us to be dissatisfied with happiness as it is commonly understood and to seek a deeper vision of flourishing or satisfaction.

The prayer is that our faith may be steadfast even when life is difficult and dark.

> *Give us the faith, O God, to walk in your ways not only when times are good but also when times are hard. Keep us steadfast when the days are dark. Anchor us securely when assailed by rumours. Help us to be generous even when we are poor, that we may witness to your eternal goodness and enjoy the pleasures of faithful living.*

This psalm challenges us to reflect on whether our desire to be happy is ambitious enough, not only for ourselves but those for whom we love.

---

121 Brueggemann and Bellinger mention this and attribute the idea to J. C. McCann Jr., p. 485.

Psalm 113: Glory above the heavens

Beginning with the word 'Hallelujah', this is the first of six psalms, known as 'the Hallel', that are recited in synagogue services at Passover. Psalm 113 is short but expansive in its vision of God's praise across all time, 'from this time forth for evermore' and across the world 'from the rising of the sun unto the going down of the same' which can be more literally translated 'from the place the sun rises to where it sets'.[122] The first half of the psalm is focused on praise but while verse 4 acclaims the magisterial and unequalled height of God in the repetition of 'above', verse 5 says something more profoundly connecting and paradoxically praiseworthy. 'Who is like unto the Lord our God, that hath his dwelling so high : and yet humbleth himself to behold the things that are in heaven and earth?'

The remainder of the psalm goes on to identify the very things that God notices, cares about and engages with: the poor, the needy (a preferable translation to the 'simple' and the 'poor' in the Book of Common Prayer) who are in the 'dust' and 'mire', or 'refuse pile', together with childless women.

There is a dizzying yo-yoing of attention here, and it is remarkable that the psalmist attempts to take the reader's mind from the most transcendent of heights to the lowest of the low (as understood in this patriarchal context). But these intellectual and spiritual gymnastics are, as Calvin noted, for our benefit: 'God's dwelling above the heavens, at such a distance from us, does not prevent him from showing himself to be near at hand, and plainly providing for our welfare.'[123]

The prayer is one of praise to the God who visits and transforms those whom the world has left behind.

> *Blessed be God! We seek you beyond the heavens and yet find you bringing fulfilment, dignity and joy to the forgotten and forsaken of the earth. We bless you, O God, for sharing and transforming the lives of the poor. We bless you in your glory and for your mercy, now and for ever. Blessed be God!*

This psalm is a powerful expression of the reach of God's care and love, in which language itself is stretched to show just how inclusive that love is. A relevant question for us is how we might express the extent of that reach today.

---

122 Alter, p. 403.
123 John Calvin as quoted by Brueggemann and Bellinger, p. 490.

Psalm 114: The mountains skipped

This is an unusual psalm in several regards. For instance, it begins with a subordinate clause 'When Israel came out of Egypt', and incorporates taunting questions. It rushes on immediately from the exodus from Egypt and the crossing of the Red Sea, to the crossing of the River Jordan, an event that occurred 40 years later. Alongside these historical references to moments when God achieved more and more freedom for his people, there is the intermingling of what are thought by many scholars to be references to Canaanite creation mythologies.

What is clear is that this is a song of the power of God over both the created and the political orders that uses language, history and mythology to make a powerful impression on those who recite or hear the poetry. Mountains 'skip like rams' and 'little hills, like young sheep'. In the Book of Common Prayer the earth is instructed to 'tremble'. 'Tremble, thou earth, at the presence of the Lord.' But the verb translated 'tremble' might also mean 'dance', which is an image with very different resonances. In the one case the emotion is fear, in the other it is joy. The 'dance for joy' approach might render the rhetorical questions of verses 5 and 6 as friendly teases rather than mocking taunts. Christians have traditionally sung this psalm at Easter, where its blending of the recollection of exodus and the crossing of the river Jordan with the power over the created order is especially apt.

The prayer is an invitation to rejoice.

Dance and skip for joy, all creatures of the earth, sing with praise all people, for the Lord God destroys the dominion of darkness and delivers us from all that is evil. Dance and skip for joy, all the whole earth, for the Lord God frees the captives, redeems the righteous, and calls all people to share the delights of eternal life.

This dense and unusual psalm brims with energy and the invitation to respond is quite natural. Whether we should quake with fear or dance for joy is a real question; but maybe the ambiguity is apposite and we should do both.

Psalm 115: Trust in the Lord

Like Psalm 114, this is a psalm with unusual features from the outset. For instance, no other psalm begins with a negative, 'Not unto us, O Lord, not unto us.' It is a psalm that is hard to categorize and keeps changing its perspective, sometimes addressing God but then quickly switching to the people.

Also, like Psalm 114, it echoes a taunting question. The idol-worshipers derive confidence from being able to see their gods. The problem, however, is that these material deities are inert. Mockery of their lack of agency leads to the psycho-theological insights that, 'They that make them are like unto them : and so are all such as put their trust in them.' Surprisingly, perhaps, it's the invisible God who is powerful and active and therefore trustworthy. This is why everyone is enjoined to trust the Lord. And the point is made that the God who remembers, or is 'mindful', shall reward such trust with blessings and a fruitful future.

The psalm ends with a brief description of a three-tier universe: the heavens – God's place, the earth – our place, and underneath – the dead who are as inert as the idols previously mentioned. It is all rounded off with a commitment to praise God 'from this time forth for evermore'. And the final word is 'Hallelujah!', 'Praise the Lord.'

The prayer is that we may turn to God.

Turn us, O God, from trust in our own efforts to trust in your love. Turn us from the worship of the worthless to the worship of you. Turn us from all that drains our energy to pursuits that enliven us and enrich our communities. Turn us back to you, O God, that we may live well, trust the trustworthy and worship wisely.

The idea that we come to resemble what we worship is one reason why we must not settle for poor theology. For what we will come to resemble is not the pure nature of God but our own inevitably inadequate understanding of God.

Psalm 116: Trouble and heaviness

The first line of Psalm 116 in the Prayer Book translation is very idiosyncratic; 'I am well pleased' is elsewhere widely rendered 'I love the Lord.' Either way, the opening certainly suggests that the psalm is a personal statement. Reading on, we discover that there is a context for this attitude of love towards God. It seems that the poet has encountered either great danger, or, and this is perhaps more likely, a life-threatening condition or illness. 'The snares of death compassed me round about : and the pains of hell gat hold upon me.'

Readers of the psalm might be reminded of the fourteenth century visionary and theologian, Julian of Norwich. Julian experienced her visions or 'revelations' when or shortly after, she was extremely close to death. The impact of the experience was so profound that she not only wrote it up but then spent 20 years meditating on it all before writing it up again, at considerably greater length. Quite how long the psalmist spent reflecting before offering this psalm in response to their experience is not clear.

Towards the end of the psalm, the writer asks what might be done to repay their debt of gratitude to God. The answer suggests continuing to 'call upon' God, pay 'vows', and offer 'the sacrifice of thanksgiving' as well as accepting both the status of a servant and the gift of freedom. The relationship has moved on quickly from unilateral rescue to a more nuanced and dynamic mutuality that culminates in praise.

The prayer is that remembrance of difficulties overcome might strengthen our faith.

Accept our thanks, good Lord, as we recall the dangers we have survived and the diseases from which we have been healed. Help us to remember our difficult days with the calm gratitude that flows from faith and comes to fulfilment in heartfelt praise.

We respond to difficult experiences in a variety of ways. We might try to forget them, we might grumble about them, or we might explain them away. The deeper challenge is to try meet God in the actuality of our experience, however difficult.

Psalm 117: The truth of the Lord

Not only the shortest psalm but the shortest chapter in the Bible, the few words of Psalm 117 are remarkably expansive. It is an invitation to praise the Lord, extended not just to the people of Israel but to 'all ye heathen ... all ye nations'. Paul quotes it towards the end of his epistle to the Romans to complete his argument that the gospel is for all.[124]

Verse 2 gives the most succinct of all possible reasons that might be adduced for this expansive directive. At its heart is the idea that God is kind, loving and merciful, but there is more than that here. God's kindness is not 'niceness'; it is a massively powerful force, more than capable of dealing with anything that might obstruct its way. This is difficult to render into English, perhaps because our language doesn't really accept the notion that kindness is a force. But the idea is there in the Prayer Book's words 'more and more' which is simply rendered 'great' in a modern translation.[125] Alter's translation reads, 'His kindness overwhelms us.'[126] The poetic parallel is that the Lord's truth has no temporal limit, 'the truth of the Lord endureth for ever'. And all this leads up to the familiar ending in the Hallel psalms, the shout of 'Hallelujah'.

The prayer is only a little shorter than the psalm itself, and seeks to do the same job.

> *We praise thee with one voice, O God, because we are overwhelmed by the power of thy mercy, thy kindness, thy love, and the beauty of thy truth. Alleluia.*

The idea that there is power in kindness is itself powerful, but the thought that it could be overwhelming may not be comfortable. But isn't kindness always good?

---

124 Romans 15.11.
125 NRSV.
126 Alter, p. 414.

Psalm 118: The gate of the Lord

It is helpful to observe from the outset that the first and final verses of Psalm 118 are identical invitations to praise, thank or acclaim God on account of God's mercy, love and kindness. Scholars believe that the song was used liturgically, like the other Hallel psalms, and that the references to entering through gates and binding the sacrifice with cords 'yea, even unto the horns of the altar' suggest a procession. No wonder, then, that all the evangelists quoted this psalm when describing Jesus' entry into Jerusalem. Indeed, the word 'hosanna', meaning 'save us', is hidden in this translation in verse 25: 'Help me now, O Lord.' And the following verse is used too, 'Blessed be he that cometh in the name of the Lord' and this not only in the gospels but also in the Benedictus of the Mass.

Some see this psalm as a compilation, while others see it as a carefully crafted celebration of rescue. It could, of course, be both. It certainly begins with a very strong affirmation of God's enduring mercy, or, as modern translations have it, God's 'steadfast love' before recalling a variety of difficult occasions that were addressed by faith and trust in God. As it goes on, God is praised more and more positively (see verses 14 and 15) and the virtue of faithfulness is extolled with growing conviction. This fits with the idea that it is a song sung in procession of increasing intensity to a holy site, though it might also be reasonable to conjecture that such a song might also be sung when the pilgrims have returned to their homes to rekindle the memory.

The prayer is that we might be merciful, kind and loyal.

O God of mercy, make us merciful; O God of kindness, make us kind; O God of loyalty, let us be loyal and faithful in all we do, singing thy praise, and trusting in thee whatever trouble afflicts us or danger threatens our homes, our friends or our community.

Singing together can be such a powerful experience – deepening emotion and strengthening community – that it is difficult to imagine a religion where there is no singing. To what extent has your spirituality been shaped by what you have sung?

Psalm 119: Walk in the law

The longest psalm, and the longest chapter in the Bible, Psalm 119 is an especially challenging text when read in English or any other modern language. This is because, unlike the second longest, Psalm 78, which is a saga in verse, but like a number of shorter psalms, it has an acrostic pattern. Uniquely, however, in this psalm each letter of the Hebrew alphabet begins not just one verse or half verse, but eight consecutive verses. This is why it divides so neatly into 22 eight-verse sections.[127] Such a form is impossible to render in translation where there is no obvious explanation for the psalm's non-narrative and non-linear style and the basis of its mnemonic power is lost.

However, once the reader is aware of this background it is possible to read, say, sing or hear the psalm with greater appreciation for what it actually is: a celebration of the Torah and all it represents and enables. But translation is an issue even here, because the word 'torah' means both 'the first five books of the bible' and 'the wisdom that they encapsulate'. We, however, collapse all this into the word 'law'. This causes two problems. First, the word 'law' in English means something much more precise and prescriptive than torah; and second that 'law' is negatively contrasted with 'grace' in the New Testament.[128] The psalmist simply doesn't think in terms of such a clear distinction as we can see when Psalm 118, all about grace, and Psalm 119, all about law, are placed side by side but with no sense of tension, never mind contradiction. As the very first verse puts it, 'Blessed are those that are undefiled in the way : and walk in the law of the Lord'. The 'way' of God, in parallel with the 'law', is life-giving in the richest possible sense. 'Law' here is an extremely positive concept, aimed at facilitating fullness of life. The first half of the penultimate verse might then summarize the spirit of this spectacular psalm: 'O let my soul live, and it shall praise thee.'

The prayer is that we might live in God's way.

Nourish us, O God, through the study of your word and your teaching. Draw us back to your way when we go astray. Return us to diligence when we neglect our studies or our prayers, and make us wise enough to continue to seek your wisdom as long as we live.

The idea that we might flourish and be blessed by obeying the law is a challenging one to us. This is in good part explained by developing our understanding of law as torah, but is there not also scope to think more widely about what obedience means?

---

127 It is also why it is 176 verses long: 8 x 22 = 176.
128 See also the discussion of Torah in the introductory essay 'Praying with the Psalms' pp xv–xvii.

Psalm 120: Woe is me

Psalm 120 is the first of 15 that have the superscription 'A Song of Ascents'. Most scholars believe that these have their origin as pilgrim songs that were sung by those making their way towards the temple in Jerusalem. They are all quite short and have some vivid and concrete images. Psalm 120 is the prayer offered by someone who is distressed by what people have been saying, and so the poet prays to be delivered from 'lying lips' and 'a deceitful tongue'. Although the matter is apparently being handed over to God in prayer, the petitioner does not hesitate to state what they believe would be appropriate retribution for the malicious slanderer, 'mighty and sharp arrows, with hot burning coals'. Whether this is someone getting something off their chest or a fully intended petition, it is worth noting that there is some poetry in the exasperated cry, as 'malicious words' are elsewhere likened to 'arrows'.

The second half of the psalm broadens the scope of the complaint. The problem is not just that one or two people are bad-mouthing the poet, but that they feel quite ill-at-ease in the community. The references to Mesech and Kedar are rhetorical. The writer doesn't live *in* such alien places, but among people who are alien and alienating. The psalmist is experiencing the familiar as strange and uncomfortable. The efforts of the psalmist to reach out peacefully are rebuffed. In short, this is the prayer of a person who is friendless in their own hometown.

The prayer is for all who feel they don't belong.

Hear our prayer, good Lord, for all who are ill at ease at home or who are not at one with the people of their neighbourhood. We pray for all who feel alienated from their colleagues at work, and all who feel distant from the people of their hometown. Bless them and bless us with a renewed sense of acceptance and belonging, that we may enjoy our circumstances in life and contribute to the common good.

Communities and homes don't just happen, they are made, and often they are 'works in progress'. This psalm might prompt us to ask what we might do to make our community more of a community and our home more of a home.

Psalm 121:Thy keeper[129]

Unusually, this psalm begins with a question, 'from whence cometh my help?', meaning 'where will I find help?' The context is a threatening mountain range; taken to represent all the dangers of life but also perhaps the specific dangers of those who are travelling. If the 'pilgrimage theory' of the Songs of Ascent is correct, these would be hills crossed on the way to Jerusalem. The faith expressed here is that it is God who provides the help when walking through the mountains.

The rest of the psalm enriches this basic understanding, and refers to the Lord's vigilant 'keeping' of his people 'Behold, he that keepeth Israel : shall neither slumber nor sleep.' The Lord is a 'defence' (some translations have 'shade'), 'So that the sun shall not burn thee by day : neither the moon by night.' The sun and moon are not meant literally (whoever heard of moonburn?) but are here poetic representations of the various threats of day and night.

Of particular interest throughout the psalm is the repeated reassurance of the Lord's intention and ability to 'keep', which is somewhat lost in the use of the word 'preserve' in the Book of Common Prayer in the final verses. There is an echo here of the Aaronic blessing 'the Lord bless you and keep you' (Numbers 6.24–26). There is a sense of kindly sustaining here, and of 'remaining with'. These are more suitable images than 'preserving', a word whose connections with pickling vegetables or canning fruit are unhelpful.

The psalm is about God's ability to help, and God's intention to stay with us and to respond to us now with our best interests at heart and with the (very) long-view in mind: 'from this time forth for evermore'.

The prayer is that God will keep us safe in the many circumstances of everyday life.

Keep us safe, O God, as we encounter threat and danger on our journey through life. Be with us by day and by night, when we are in company and when we are alone. Be with us at work and when we are at rest, when we are at leisure and when we are under pressure to respond to life's more difficult challenges. Keep us safe, O God, now and always.

The question of God's long-term interest in us is a deep and ancient one and yet can be lost in a world where attention spans are getting shorter. Can we even imagine God's attention span?

---

129 Psalms 121–134 are collectively known as the 'Songs of Ascent'. These are believed to have originated as the songs of pilgrims approaching and entering Jerusalem. They are some of the more immediately accessible psalms. As Thomas Merton has written, 'Perhaps these short, joyful songs are the most beautiful in the whole Psalter. They are full of light and confidence. They bring God very close to us. They open our hearts to the secret action of His peace and to His silent grace.' Merton, p. 21

Psalm 122: The peace of Jerusalem

This joyful and hopeful psalm is located on the edge of the walled city of Jerusalem. The pilgrims are at last on the threshold of their destination, and their imaginations are synthesizing the reality of the great city with the even greater hopes that the word 'Jerusalem' enshrines. Among them is the hope of peace, as the word 'Jerusalem' carries within it the word 'shalom'. But more than peace is being sought and celebrated here. 'Jerusalem' means place of worship and unity, but also place of justice and truth.

The vision of Jerusalem as the epicenter of the world – represented perhaps to the rather self-pleased amusement of our modern minds in medieval maps, such as the Mappa Mundi – is rooted not in poor geography, but in prophetic utterances such as that of Isaiah.

> For out of Zion shall go forth instruction,
>   and the word of the Lord from Jerusalem.
> He shall judge between the nations,
>   and shall arbitrate for many peoples;
> they shall beat their swords into ploughshares,
>   and their spears into pruning-hooks;
> nation shall not lift up sword against nation,
>   neither shall they learn war any more. (Isaiah 2.3b–4)

The vision is not of world domination nor ethnic or religious exclusion but of inclusion under beneficent rule of God. Human community is historically viable and sustainable when the hope of harmonious peace is actively pursued. That such a vision is contradicted by daily reality is all the more reason to pray for its realization.

The prayer is for those who carry responsibility for religious leadership.

O Lord God, imbue those who pray with loving and peaceful hearts, that all people of faith might avoid destructive attitudes and spurn the paths of violence and mutual hatred. Bless all religious leaders with genuine humility and with the nobility of character that fosters harmony and seeks the good of all, that the great religions of the world might lead humanity towards the new Jerusalem and the time of justice and peace foretold by the prophets.

This way of thinking about Jerusalem is also a way of trying to represent and focus our sense of ultimate destination or destiny. What might be a way to represent the confluence of our noblest hopes and best values today?

Psalm 123: We are utterly despised

Short, intimate and telling, Psalm 123 is a poem that expresses deep longing for God's relief from the pain of being exposed to the most corrosive of attitudes: 'Have mercy upon us, O Lord, have mercy upon us : for we are utterly despised.' The final verse amplifies this, speaking of 'the scornful reproof of the wealthy' and 'the despitefulness of the proud'. The poet here has 'had enough', is 'sated'[130] with contempt or disrespect.

One way of looking at the psalm is as 'the voice of a servant class'.[131] This view is supported by the language of verse 2, which suggests that the writer is accustomed to adopting the patient attentiveness of one who waits on another, and sees this as the right stance to have before God. This, however, could be a product of imagination or observation just as easily as a reflection of experience. The real focus of the psalm is the resentment of the scorn and contempt that the poet experiences from those who are rich, complacent, proud and 'haughty'.[132] Such attitudes can be psychologically toxic. Communities and groups can survive many crises but that the problems caused by contempt can be among the most difficult for them to bear.

The prayer is for those who are on the receiving end of contempt.

Look with great kindness, O God, on all who experience the insult and degradation of contempt or disrespect. Embrace them in your loving arms and send them understanding counsellors and strong advocates. Touch the eyes of those who look down on others, that they may see the dignity and beauty of your image in those whom they disdain; turn their hearts, we pray, that repenting of their sins, they may offer to others the respect and honour they deserve.

Being in receipt of contempt is one of life's more extreme social and spiritual challenges, but there is an even subtler one: to become aware of the extent to which we ourselves have contempt for others. The challenge here is two-edged.

---

130 Alter's word, p. 441.
131 Brueggemann and Bellinger, p. 532.
132 Alter's word, p. 442.

Psalm 124: The snare is broken

This is a song of collective thanksgiving, sung by the community together and encouraged by a leader, who would have called out the words 'now may Israel say' to encourage participation. It recalls days of dark danger, where, but for the Lord's help, the people would soon have been defeated: 'They had swallowed us up quick' means 'they would have eaten us alive'.

Further disasters are imagined, mostly associated with being deluged, 'The deep waters of the proud : had gone even over our soul.' The wording of Coverdale's translation makes it seem that these imagined events had actually happened. The reality is that this not a psalm of lament or complaint but a 'psalm of thanksgiving' that expresses the thought, 'Yes, that was bad, but actually it could have been much worse.' The key comes towards the end, 'But praised be the Lord : who hath not given us over for a prey unto their teeth', and there follows the beautiful and vivid image of the escape and deliverance of the soul, 'even as a bird out of the snare of the fowler'.

The final verse reiterates the familiar thought in the psalms that, 'Our help standeth in the Name of the Lord : who hath made heaven and earth.' It connects the magnificent work of creating all that is with the detailed care of God's beloved people. The dialectic between the massive and the micro is typical of the spirituality expressed in the psalms. That God can and does relate and act at both extremes, and at all levels in between, is intrinsic to the Judeo-Christian understanding of God.

The prayer is for those who have been rescued and those who have rescued them.

We give you thanks, good Lord, for all who have recently been brought to safety from the midst of catastrophe: those rescued from flooded homes, those saved from a storm at sea, those who have been dug from the earth after an earthquake or from snow after an avalanche, those pulled from a burning building or vehicle, those sped to a safe haven from a forest fire. We give thanks for their good fortune and pray with gratitude for the skill and dedication of those who risk their own lives to save others.

Connecting the help that God gives to God's status and work as creator is a rhetorical way to reinforce the sense of God's power. But might it be that God's healing is actually best understood as an extension of God's creating?

Psalm 125: The lot of the righteous

Psalm 125 begins with two powerful and parallel similes: the faithful are like 'mount Sion' and the Lord surrounds his people even as 'The hills stand about Jerusalem.' The opening thus conveys reasons to be faithful and trusting and to accept that God's powerful love and protection are given unreservedly and not as a reward. This is a Jerusalem psalm, like others in this section, but this one relates back especially closely to the strong sense of security expressed in Psalm 46. Or so it is in verses 1–3, the third especially asserting the reliability of God's protection against enemies.

The final two verses seem to offer a different theology. One not of unconditional and proactive mercy, but of just deserts, 'Do well, O Lord : unto those that are good and true of heart.' In a contemporary idiom this verse might read, 'respond with grace to those who have integrity'. At the end of the psalm it is clear that those who turn back (or aside) from God's way will be counted and treated as they evildoers they are. 'But those who turn aside to their / own crooked ways / the Lord will lead away with evildoers.' [133] Far from being 'unconditional', this reads very much like the law of moral cause and effect.

The very final words, although somewhat appended to a verse that seems complete already, are nonetheless comforting for the people as a whole, 'but peace shall be upon Israel'.

The prayer is for integrity.

Shape our attitudes, O God, form our minds, and mold our hearts, that we may be at one with your will and your way. Give us integrity in our thoughts and in our words, in our feelings and in our actions, and draw us towards the authenticity of spirit that reflects your grace, your love and your truth.

Integrity is a highly prized quality today and we are certainly drawn to people who appear authentic or show sincerity. How do these values relate to those such as happiness, flourishing and fulfilment?

---

133 NRSV. Alter uses the phrase 'those who bend to crookedness', p. 446.

Psalm 126: We rejoice

This psalm represents a quest to discover an appropriate way to express the happiness and joy that come from imagining and experiencing the loving restoration of good fortune and favour achieved by God. Unfortunately, Coverdale selects the word 'captivity' and uses it twice. This is a mistranslation that turns the meaning of the psalm from one of restoration of fortune to the 'turning' of 'captivity'. It's not the worst possible mistake to make, because the Lord is the great liberator. But it is the restoration of fortune that seems so wonderful that the people feel it is a 'dream' and recall, 'Then was our mouth filled with laughter : and our tongue with joy.'

The recollection of such restoration dominates the first half of the psalm, but the second half is framed by the petition in verse 5. As the NRSV puts it, 'Restore our fortunes, O Lord.' 'The rivers in the south' mentioned in the same verse, also need a comment as these 'rivers' are in fact wadis or dry pools of the Negeb that are filled by seasonal rains.[134]

The final two verses use the agricultural process of sowing and reaping to suggest a human process, under God, of mourning and sadness that gives way to rejoicing. The psalm is in effect a prayer that this recollected process may become a reality once again and the people's fortunes restored.

The prayer is that our best memories may equip us with hope for the future.

> *Bless us, O God, with pleasure, joy and delight when we recall the days in the past when we were happy and fulfilled, confident and secure; and on our difficult days, when we are disoriented by events and when plans for the future suddenly seem vain, bless us with renewed hope, fresh courage and the gift of faith. Do not let the uncertainties of life make us anxious, but allow them to open our hearts to your guidance, your grace and to the future that your providence has prepared for us.*

Meditating on this psalm we may find ourselves asking whether the joyful recollection of restored fortune in the past is a good-enough basis to pray for restored fortune in the future.

---

134 Alter, p. 448.

Psalm 127: He giveth his beloved sleep

'Except', 'Unless' – these are not the words that we normally find at the beginning of a psalm and they indicate that a subtle thought is about to be articulated. And the thought is not that it's wrong to work hard, or to seek to achieve, or to build houses, or even to develop whole cities or even civilizations. None of these projects are deprecated here. Effort and achievement can be good. However, they can also be 'vain' and labour is sometimes 'lost'. As we make our plans and put in our efforts, we need to discern whether or not our project is 'of God'.

Verse 3 is a 'wake-up call' (though a better metaphor might be a 'take-a-rest call') to all who find themselves working to excess. The value of sleep is affirmed. It is a blessing to those who are beloved of God. To take healthy rest is not to indulge in the sin of sloth. Rest is a good part of life and essential to a good life. Indeed, without rest, without stepping back from the fray, it is hard to imagine any sensible 'discernment' being part of our planning.

The second half of the psalm begins with verse 4, which introduces a completely unexpected thought, which is that children are both a 'heritage' and 'gift'. One child is good, but many are better and what we are presented with here is basically an inducement to breed. The sentiments in the last verse may strike us as at best archaic. Few today would think of their children as potential militia to see off enemies at the gate. And yet are not children potentially the guardians of a future that might otherwise be lonely and vulnerable? And besides, this is poetry, not argument. The most important word in the final verse is the first one, 'happy'.

The prayer is that our work might be blessed.

Bless our efforts, O Lord, not because they are great but because they are guided by your purposes. Bless our actions, not because they are relentless but because they are careful. Bless our projects, not because they are grand but because they will benefit others; and bless us with the full appreciation of all that we have been given by your grace.

This psalm invites us to recognize that we have profoundly influenced others, certainly those whom we have brought into the world, but also others whom we have nurtured or educated or in some way shaped. Who comes to mind?

Psalm 128: O well is thee

Like Psalm 1, Psalm 128 spells out the benefits of living a godly life. In this case it is the wisdom of fearing the Lord and walking 'in his ways' that are praised, and which will be rewarded with happiness. It is a 'beatitude psalm' that reflects the themes and concerns of all biblical wisdom literature. The form that the blessings take is domestic and patriarchal. The blessed man enjoys the fruits of his own labour, has a 'fruitful' wife tucked away 'in the recesses of the house',[135] and has plenty of children and grandchildren – together with the longevity to see and enjoy it all. On a somewhat wider scale, there is the hope of 'prosperity' for Jerusalem, which one might think of as the good of the whole community, and there is a promise of peace for all the people of God.

It is hard to engage with this psalm without having some sort of reaction to the palpable patriarchy, but maybe it is possible to get beyond that and read it at another level. Namely, that the point about being in receipt of God's blessing is not that ordinary life has something special added, not that there is some kind of spiritual bonus, or a dividend on life for the faithful, but that for the faithful ordinary life is itself satisfying, productive and sustainable. What is ordinary and normal will change from generation to generation, but the psalm is helpful in drawing attention to the importance of daily domestic life, even though it also has the potential to perpetuate norms that contradict the psalmic priority of social justice.

The prayer is for fulfilment and contentment.

Help us, O God of blessings, to live in accord with your will and to walk in your ways, that we may find fulfilment in all that we have received, and contentment in the circumstances of our daily lives.

The question of the way in which our domestic life is ordered is forced to the surface by this psalm. It invites us to reflect on what blessing and beatitude look like for everyone at home.

---

135 Alter's phrase, p. 452.

Psalm 129: They vexed me

Psalm 129 carries the memory of violence. It is the song of one who has been ill-used by those with power. '[F]ought against me' and 'vexed me' don't have the same sense of 'attack' or even bullying that more contemporary translators invoke, and that's unfortunate. This psalm is not about friends scrapping; it's about being picked on. It is Israel that is making the protest; the whole nation is unhappy.

The image in verse 3 of a plough raking across the back is gruesome, and calls to mind the lashing meted out to Jesus and the flogging of St Paul. J. S. Bach has Jesus' bloodied back transfigured to a rainbow in the St John Passion, but there is no mystical transformation of suffering, or its vindication, here. Verse 4 is a little cryptic, but the meaning is that God actually prevents the worst excesses of physical violence and abuse by disconnecting the plowers from their ploughs.

The rest of the psalm is a plea for just desserts for those who have inflicted the violence; that the bullies will get their comeuppance. Not the grandest or most noble of sentiments, perhaps, but we don't come to the psalms for ethical elegance. Rather we turn to them for honesty and realism and guidance in bringing as much of life as possible to God's attention. With the psalmist for a guide, the bullied and abused will call out those who harm them, and express both the depth of their own suffering and their desire for justice to 'the righteous Lord'. In short, they will put their future in God's hands.

While the words of this psalm are harsh it can be remembered that they are words and not deeds; they are a way of speaking rather than a way of doing, and by speaking in this way before God the hope is that we might be led to actions that are less violent than our words.

The prayer is that we move towards forgiving those who have harmed us.

Help us, O God, to live calmly with the memories from our younger years that still cause us distress. Help us, in particular, to live with the recollection of the individuals who have harmed us. As we thank you for the freedom that we have gained from the actual harm that was once our regular experience, give us the grace to be able to think of those who hurt us without ill-will or bitterness.

The question of how we carry the memory of violence or abuse is a current one as well as an ancient one. Are we any wiser than our ancestors in dealing with this particular issue?

Psalm 130: Out of the deep

Psalm 130 is the prayer of someone whose life has fallen apart. '[T]he deep' is the low emotional level to which the person has sunk, and the feeling at the beginning of the poem is that the speaker has lost all confidence, they cannot even dare to hope that they will ever be heard. The experience is one that many can resonate with, not as the way things always are, but as the way in which they can be from time to time. Such, perhaps, are our worst days, and one reason why this psalm is well known is that it is when life is most difficult that we need help to pray.

The depths here are not, however, the depths of suffering inflicted on us by others. This is a situation of personal culpability with a plea for clemency mixed in. This serves as a bold introduction to the following verse where it is remembered that 'there is mercy with thee'. While the Book of Common Prayer has this as a cause of 'fear', contemporary ears might find it more helpful to hear from modern translators that this is a reason for God to be 'revered'.[136]

The Psalm is dense indeed and quickly moves on to another profound spiritual theme, that of waiting. 'I look for the Lord; my soul doth wait for him.' There is an intensity of spiritual desire caught up in this, which reflects the starting point, where the speaker is languishing in a pit that is of their own making. But now there is hope and expectation. 'It's dark down here, but the dawn will come.' That's a metaphorical faith statement rather than a scientific fact, as this is a poem and a prayer and not a treatise on the reliability of the cycle of daily time.

The psalm ends with an invitation to all God's people to put their hope in God's redemptive intentions.

The prayer is that we may trust God even when close to despair.

Help us to trust in you, O God, when we are in trouble, even when the trouble is of our own making. Be our light in the darkness. Be our patience in times of frustration. Be our comfort when we despair. Be the support that secures us when we struggle. We call out from the deep, O God, reach to us from on high.

That actions of others hurt us and put us in need is well understood. That we inadvertently and unwittingly harm ourselves is harder to accept, perhaps because it takes us to a deeper and darker place of self-awareness.

---

136 NRSV.

Psalm 131: As a weaned child

The opening of this short psalm is arresting and unusual, 'Lord, I am not high-minded : I have no proud looks'. It introduces a three-fold negative assertion that adds up to a version of humility that veers towards the abject. It enshrines somewhat uncomfortably the paradox of boasting about humility which, if we are not circumspect, might lead us up the spiritual and ethical cul-de-sac of praising ourselves for our lack of ambition, or even for our failure to take responsibility.

An image that comes in the second half of verse 3, that of a weaned child, is puzzling but also promising. The picture here is not so much of lowliness as of contentment. The idea is not that the speaker or reader is a baby in the sense of being helplessly immature, but in the sense of being in the immediate and comforting presence of strong and reliable maternal love and protection.

The image of the weaned child might perhaps stimulate the Christian reader to think of a Madonna with the infant Christ. The contentment here is mutual. The humility and lowliness of the child is for the benefit of the mother and the humility and lowliness of the mother is for the benefit of the whole human race. Mutual trust is hugely important if people are to be content together, and it is with a sense of the enduring importance of trust that this short psalm ends. It is trust in God that is central and both makes for, and requires, genuine humility.

The prayer is that by humility and trust God may lead us to true contentment.

Draw us, O Lord, ever closer to your love, that we may come to know true contentment and abiding peace. When we are too proud to seek your love, gently humble us. When we are too nervous, quickly calm us. When we are too anxious to let go of our concerns, give us the grace to trust in you, that in humility, and with contentment and trust, we may witness to your enduring kindness and love.

What is at issue in this psalm is not how we can make ourselves admirably humble by refusing to take adult responsibilities seriously, but the question of how we can, as responsible adults, experience contentment in the presence of God.

Psalm 132: My rest for ever

Psalm 132 celebrates the achievements of David in finding the Ark of the Covenant and establishing Jerusalem, or Sion (in verse 14) as God's city. The events to which it refers are narrated in 2 Samuel 6–7. It is a poem in two halves, the first of which is framed by the petitions in verses 1 and 10, 'Lord, remember David : and all his trouble' and 'turn not away the presence of thine Anointed'. The point being referenced here is the strenuous and relentless effort that David made to find and deliver the Ark of the Covenant.

The second half of the psalm is God's response to David, which takes the form of a vow to ensure that David's line, if it remains faithful, will retain the kingship. The picture that follows is of the quality of life in the holy city when it is both God's residence and presided over by a good ruler. There is hospitality, there is good religion in the form of priests now being able to do what they should do, and people being filled with joy at the celebrations. On the practical side, there are ample provisions for all, while politically it goes well for the king and badly for the king's enemies.

The prayer is for those offering public ministry today.

Bless, O Lord, all who have been anointed to serve you as a minster of your people and as a herald of your kingdom. Clothe them with humility, guide them towards justice, nurture them in truth, and fill their hearts with love. Strengthen and direct them when they are in trouble, do not turn away from them when they need comfort; and give them vitality and health, that they may flourish in bringing many others to the joyful peace of knowing your love and serving your will.

This psalm is infused with a deep desire for settled faith, political stability and domestic security. These are perennial concerns, but what spiritual longings are uppermost today?

Psalm 133: Together in unity

Psalm 133 might be a pilgrim song that celebrates the reconciliation of a fractious band of travellers as they reach their destination. Certainly, the author is very happy about the unity that is being experienced, which suggests that it has not always been so and cannot be taken for granted. There is a palpable a sense of delight in the physical here, as indeed there might be after an arduous journey on foot. The symbolism of oil on the head running down over the abundant beard of Aaron is one of excess and pleasure, and possibly even fun. The poem seems to be written to communicate a mood rather than an idea, and the imagery is local particular and starkly patriarchal. We might want to experience and celebrate unity in more inclusive terms today, but that doesn't mean that we are alienated from the joy of new-found unity, however incomplete it will one day be revealed to be.

The final image of the dew of Herman irrigating the hill of Sion is a geographical impossibility that can be resolved by a small emendation of the Hebrew so that the word translated 'Sion' becomes the word translated 'parched land'.[137] The apposite beauty of the image then becomes clear. The dew is the only source of water for the land when there is no rain; it is therefore experienced as an especially delightful daily blessing. Like the oil running down Aaron's beard and over his clothing, it is guaranteed to bring a happy smile to the lips. In short, this is a joyful poem that celebrates togetherness, pleasure and flourishing.

The prayer is one that may be used before, during or after any local conflict.

Lead us, O Lord, this day and always, in the peaceful enjoyment of friendship and unity, and help us always to celebrate moments of reconciliation.

This short psalm challenges us to put a very high value on unity and to seek to become more effective in the practices of reconciliation and peacemaking.

---

137 Alter suggests this, p. 463.

Psalm 134: By night

After all the psalms of pilgrimage, this is a poem of stillness and completion. It could be thought of as the ultimate psalm of arrival. The pilgrims are in Jerusalem enjoying their first night together at the temple. They feel that there is nothing left to pray for and, as they turn to pray, they realize that the sense of God is more real than it has ever been before and that all blessing is mutual. God is named no fewer than five times in three verses; and each of those three verses includes an invitation to bless. First it is the people who must bless the Lord and then it is God who is invited to bless the people.

This was an obvious choice of a psalm for Benedict to include in the last office of the day in monastic communities, Compline, with its four short and easily remembered verses. This is a psalm in which heaven and earth touch each other with calm and warm positivity. Think of it as the basis for a good night's sleep.

The prayer is for the end of the day.

> *Bless us, O Lord, as this day ends and the night descends. Hear us as we commend to your loving care all the worries of this day and all our hopes for the future, and, as we seek your blessing, let us offer you our thanks and our praise, our thanks and our praise.*[138]

Rote learning has been out of favour as an educational tool for many decades. But might there be value in committing the words of this psalm to memory, of learning it 'by heart'.

---

138 Especially if used late at night, the final words may be repeated as a mantra, 'our thanks and our praise, our thanks and our praise, our thanks and our praise ...'

Psalm 135: Sing praises unto his name

This psalm is a powerful, richly-packed and tightly-constructed song in praise of Yahweh, the Lord, the God of Israel. It begins and ends with an invitation to people and priests to join together in this act of praise, which is a response to the lively and redeeming power of God. God is super-powerful and God 'hath chosen Jacob unto himself : and Israel for his own possession'. The praise of God, and God's mastery over creation, is thus caught up with the joy of being God's people and celebrating the power that God has exercised in delivering them from slavery and establishing a new place for them. 'He smote divers nations : and slew mighty kings.'

In words that we first came across in Psalm 115, the gods of the other nations are derided for their lack of life and power: 'They have mouths, and speak not : eyes have they, but they see not.' Moreover, their makers and worshippers are taunted because their practices only serve to limit their capacities, 'They that make them are like unto them : and so are all they that put their trust in them.' Such derision is the flip-side of the praise of the God who is the powerful, partisan champion of the chosen people, who, priests and people alike, are invited to praise. This is the God who is uniquely worthy of praise, the one who gave his name ' Yahweh' to Moses. The three final verses mirror the fulsome praise expressed in the opening three verses of the psalm.

The prayer is that our worship of God may shape our character.

O God, as we worship you, so we seek to emulate you in goodness, in grace and in service. Bless us with such qualities of character and mind that we may do your work in the world and bring honour to your name.

If those who worship idols are diminished by their practices, what might we expect to be the end of those who praise God?

Psalm 136: Great wonders

Whereas Psalm 135 was a powerful song of praise, Psalm 136 is a relentless song of thanksgiving. Yahweh, the Lord, is the God of all gods – a phrase that implies the superlative, Yahweh is the 'greatest God'.[139] The structure of this psalm is extremely simple. Each verse identifies a historical moment that is worth remembering gratefully, attributes it to God's action, and follows it with the refrain 'for his mercy endureth for ever'. Alter translates this as 'for His kindness is forever', and suggests that it must have been a response by the people in a liturgy.[140] The emphasis of the phrase is on the enduring, timeless, reliable nature of God's 'kindness'. In his transliteration, Peterson uses the idiomatic 'his love never quits',[141] which in its punchy way points to the distinctive spirituality of this psalm.

The historical moments related are familiar and begin with creation before moving on to liberation from slavery in Egypt, the passage through the wilderness, victory over the kingdoms beyond the Jordan and, in the final verses, occasions when Israel was in trouble, delivered from enemies and given food. The whole psalm comes to a grand conclusion as God is thanked for being God.

The extensive nature of the litany is impressive, possibly even overpowering, but the most striking aspect of the psalm is not the litany so much as the pulse-beat of the refrain. The message is a strong one; life works out well because God never quits.

The prayer is a short thanksgiving.

O God, the creator of all that is good, the inspiration of all that is wonderful, the champion of the poor, the liberator of slaves, and the power that brings good out of evil, hear us now as we give offer our fulsome thanks and our endless praise.

This psalm uses the power of repetition to create a sense of community, identity and history as well as of thanksgiving. The psalms may reference the past, but their recitation is a practice that shapes the future.

---

139. Alter's phrase, p. 469.
140 Alter, p. 469.
141 Peterson, pp.183–5.

Psalm 137: A strange land

The suggestion that has been made several times in these pages – that it can be therapeutic to name our negativity – is certainly not proved by this psalm, ending as it does with the most distressing verse in the Bible, 'Blessed shall he be that taketh thy children : and throweth them against the stones.' This is a song of deep sadness that becomes bitterness through the act of remembering.

We might well ask what has led the poet to this apotheosis of appallingly vengeful thinking. It's clear that the context is the exile, and that the agony of remembering the days of blessing and plenty is located in some kind of camp by the waters of Babylon. But the particular point of anguish is found not in simply being there, but in the mockery that comes from the captors who, noting the lack of music in this musical people, taunt them mercilessly, demanding that they sing one of the songs of home. The taunt hurts. It prompts a rhetorical response, 'How shall we sing the Lord's song : in a strange land?' followed by a renewed loyalty for home expressed in promises never to forget its beauty and peace. But this memory brings no solace. Rather it triggers yet more grief as the traumatic days of destruction are recalled, made all the more distressing by the earworm of jeering Edomites.

This, then, is not merely a poem of loss. It is a poem of trauma. Lament it is, but 'lament' is not a sharp enough word to describe its emotional tone. It connects with the human capacity to hate, which is triggered here by violence, destruction and humiliation delivered by the deeds and words of the powerful.

The prayer is for victims of traumatic harm.

Hear us, O God, as we pray for all who have been subjected to traumatizing harm at the hands of the powerful, and all whose plight is aggravated by the taunts of their captors. Be with them in their trouble, and give them the faith, strength and courage to feel the keenness of their loss, to embrace the fury of their anger and, in time, once again to know the peace that passes all understanding.

This psalm presents a particularly difficult challenge to reflection in that its language is so stark that it puts an end to thought. And yet the deeper spiritual challenge is to learn how not to give up when our own emotions and desires are overpowering.

Psalm 138: My whole heart

Psalm 138 is considered to mark the beginning of the end of the Book of Psalms, and those that follow are seen as a summary and summation of the faith proclaimed throughout the book. It is a song of thanksgiving, which is both confident, 'even before the gods will I sing praise unto thee', and deep, as it comes from 'my whole heart'. As in many other psalms, reasons for thanks and praise are given. God is great and God's greatness is, though this sounds odd, a product of God's own agency. It is God who has 'magnified [God's] name and [God's] word above all things'. This is the God who has answered and strengthened those who have called upon God in prayer. It is clear from verse 4 that the compass of the praise of God is without limit and extends to the most powerful across the word.

Verse 6 offers a summation of Israel's faith that is seen again in Christianity, possibly in even more vivid form. This verse can be seen to anticipate the song of Mary, the second of the so-called Lucan Psalms, 'For the Lord be high, yet hath he respect unto the lowly' prefigures, 'for he hath regarded the lowliness of his handmaiden' (Luke 1.48). Also, 'as for the proud, he beholdeth them afar off' anticipates, 'and the rich he hath sent empty away' (Luke 1.53).

The Lord's guidance through times of trouble, a familiar psalmic theme, is here in condensed form, 'Though I walk in the midst of trouble, yet shalt thou refresh me', echoing words of Psalm 23. The poem concludes with the strange request that God should 'despise not then the work of thine own hands'. However, the poetic idea being expressed is not well communicated in the phrase 'despise not'. The NRSV has 'Do not forsake', and Alter suggests, 'Do not let go', as the Hebrew verb used here is associated with the slackening of the hand's grip. In short, the psalm ends with the phrase, 'don't drop your own work'.[142]

The prayer is that our confidence may be grounded in humility before God.

Remind us, O God, of your great love of the lowly and humble, that we may resist all inducement to follow the path of pride, and base our confidence in the belief that you created us, and find our purpose in sharing your life-giving loving-kindness.

Have you ever worried that God might drop you?

---

142 Alter, p. 478.

Psalm 139: Thou knowest

This psalm explodes with the poetry of intimate trust in God. 'O Lord, thou hast searched me out and known me : thou knowest my down-sitting and mine up-rising, thou understandest my thoughts long before.' In many ways this psalm is about knowing – the verb appears repeatedly. The speaker is knowingly known by God. But it is a strange knowing, a mysterious knowing, one might say. It's one thing to say that 'I know God' or that 'I have faith is God.' Such 'I' statements are the commonplace of creedal confession: 'I believe in God ...' But to say that 'God *knows* me' is another matter.

In the biblical context, 'to know' means something much richer than 'to have a notion of'. It implies intimacy and affection, possibly mutual bodily knowledge. Indeed, the way this psalm unfolds makes it clear that there is no limit to God's knowledge. There is no escaping this all-knowing God in time or in space. There is no 'before God' and there is no 'after God'; there is no place so distant that God is not there, and no darkness so deep that it is not given light by this pervasive divine presence.

There is a shadow within the psalm, however, when from verses 19 onwards, the writer turns their attention away from God and towards the wicked. The confession of hating them 'right sore' as it appears in verse 22 or 'with a perfect hatred' as a modern translation has it, pulls us up short.[143] Perhaps we should understand this as intelligent candour, full transparency, in the context of God's all-knowingness. There's no point in hiding one's feelings from the God who knows everything. And is it not often the case that we need to be clear with those we love about what we really can't stand? The psalm ends with what was declared as truth being invoked in prayer, 'search me, O God and know my heart'.[144] The parallel with verse 1 is clearer here than in the Book of Common Prayer, and so more accurately reflects the envelope structure of the psalm. The final verse is forward-looking and positive; the psalmist wants not only to be known but also to be led forward.

The prayer is that we become ever more transparent to God's love.

O God, your knowledge of my life, my feelings and my thoughts is immediate and infinite, for you have made me what I have become. Grant me such confidence in your love that I may always rejoice in your company and seek your blessing on all that I am.

The psalm encourages us by speaking of God's intimate knowledge and care for us personally, but it also challenges us to open ourselves yet more fully to the tender love of God.

---

143 NRSV.
144 NRSV.

Psalm 140: Adders' poison

Psalm 140 reflects the mind of someone whose anxiety is focused on what others will do. It starts as a prayer for deliverance from the 'evil' and the 'wicked' who not only cause trouble, but seem to delight in contemplating the mayhem they precipitate. It is a prayer for protection and the vivid and poetic nature of the language suggests that the writer has been really spooked: 'They have sharpened their tongues like a serpent : adders' poison is under their lips.' Whether this is paranoia or a response to current crisis or sustained malevolence, the feelings are genuine and the prayer is authentic. The poet remembers the times when God's protection was real, which seems to have been in a situation of actual physical threat in a time of war.

But the current situation is different; more subtle and insidious, perhaps. The threat now comes from words and attitudes, and the speaker is not so confident that protection, deliverance, or rescue will be forthcoming. Their anxiety seems never to be fully answered, but is reflected in a prayer that wicked-doers be caught in their own traps, a familiar idea in the psalms. However, in this particular case the feelings escalate, and the psalmist become more actively vengeful, ultimately praying in verse 10 that 'hot burning coals fall upon them' and that they be thrown into the fire and pit from which there is no escape.

The psalm ends with the professed belief that those who use words to attack others will not prevail, 'a man full of words will not prosper upon the earth' and that 'the Lord shall avenge the poor : and maintain the cause of the helpless.'

The final thought is that those who live well will ultimately vindicated and abide in God's presence.

The prayer is for those whose confidence is undermined by the cruel words of others.

Give us strength, O Lord, when we learn that people have spoken against us, or have used spiteful words to do us harm; shield us from the anxiety that such attacks are intended to inflict, and keep us steadfast in our efforts to be truthful, kind and respectful in our own use of language.

Psalm 140 reminds us that sometimes words or gestures or attitudes penetrate our defences, not only undermining our confidence but also provoking vengeful feelings. Why is it that cruel words can have such a profound impact on us?

Psalm 141: As the incense

This psalm contains some ideas that are familiar, together with some new imagery. It is the urgent and repeated prayer of someone who knows they are not confident that they can remain on the straight and narrow. The suggestion in verse 2 that prayer rises 'like incense' offers an interesting and helpful way of thinking about our ongoing prayer, as incense engages the sense of smell, which can be powerfully evocative of hidden feelings and important memories. When we pray there is often, perhaps, the remembrance and recollection of our former prayers so that new prayer and remembered prayer join together in our souls as a powerful offering.

The psalmist then goes on to pray that their words may be careful and that they stay away from evil actions and influences. This verse perhaps begins to anticipate the thought that is encapsulated in a petition of the Lord's Prayer – 'lead us not into temptation, but deliver us from evil' (Matthew 6.13 and Luke 11.5). The insight that we can be the cause of our own trouble is spiritually important, as is the desire for appropriate rebuke.

It is noteworthy that several body parts are mentioned through this psalm and serve to anchor it quite personally – hands, mouth and lips, heart, head, bones and eyes.

The final two verses repeat the familiar psalmic petition that the wicked fall into their own traps.

The prayer is for protection from ourselves.

Protect us, good Lord, not only from those who threaten to harm us but also from our selves. Let our hands be occupied in prayer. Let our mouths consume no more than enough. Let our lips ofer only the words of kindness. Let our heart desire only what is worthy of love. Let our heads be bowed to receive your blessing, and let our eyes be drawn to the glory of your love.

The psalm's challenge is in reminding us that trouble doesn't only come from those who wish us harm, but from within ourselves, and its advice is that we should avoid bad influences and seek out good ones.

Psalm 142: My spirit was in heaviness

The beginning of the final verse is important to any reading of this psalm, 'Bring my soul out of prison.' Traditionally associated with the occasion when David was in a cave hiding from Saul (1 Samuel 24), the psalm is relevant and realistic both to those who are literally incarcerated and to those for whom 'being in prison' is a metaphor for their feelings.

The idea that this is a metaphorical prison, or perhaps a hiding place, makes sense in terms of some of the sentiments expressed earlier in the poem. The plaintiff soul looks for help but finds none, can't find a place to 'flee unto', is without personal care and apparently has powerful persecutors. All these realities shape the prayer of the psalmist who doesn't whisper vague requests but makes a hearty cry and pours out complaints. A trap has been set. At the end there is hopeful vision of living well, socializing with the righteous and giving thanks to God.

The point at issue in the psalm is not therefore whether the psalmist was really in prison, or whether they will ever really come to enjoy a good life, but how hope of transformation is born. And the answer to that seems to be that the midwife of true hope is honest and heartfelt prayer, reflecting the way things actually are and how they really feel.

The prayer is for the forlorn.

Help us, O Lord, in our most forlorn moments and on our most desperate days to call for your help and seek your aid, and then to continue to seek it, even when we fear that our prayer cannot be heard. Help us to whisper our prayer when we are isolated, and to cry it aloud when surrounded by those who intend us harm, that we may once again know the reassurance of your loving-kindness and the comfort of good companions.

The psalms invite us to embrace the emotional risk of overcoming denial about our problems, so that we might 'say it as it is' in our prayers and be brought to wholeness and newness of life. The challenge is to identify and name our own denial.

Psalm 143: I flee unto thee

Verse 4 of Psalm 143 gives us the starting point, 'Therefore is my spirit vexed within me'. More recent translations say that the spirit 'faints', but 'vexation' is a helpfully strong word, referring to the frustrated and irritated kind of worry that is further irked by triviality. It isn't much used today, but nonetheless points to the sort of experience that this psalm works with. It starts with supplication, and expresses spiritual modesty. Verse 2, 'And enter not into judgement with thy servant : for in thy sight shall no man living be justified', is as good a statement of the way in which any human being would wisely approach the judgement of grace as can be found anywhere in the Bible.

The problem with which this psalm wrestles is not, however, primarily internal or subjective. The poet has been persecuted by an enemy. The prayer that this leads to includes remembrance, intensification of petition and the expression of intention and desire to do God's will, or, in Coverdale's words, 'to do the thing that pleaseth thee'. Maybe a radical change of life is needed here.

The Psalm ends with a prayer for preservation of life itself, things really are desperate, and a plea for rescue from danger. The final note is fierce. 'And of thy goodness slay mine enemies : and destroy all them that vex my soul.' That word 'vex' again – more recent translations don't have the circumlocution but refer straightforwardly and bluntly to 'enemies' or 'adversaries'.

The prayer is that we may be able to face life's challenges with helpful emotions.

Calm us, O God, when afflicted by anxiety and irritation, and help us always to come to a good judgement of the severity of any threat that we face. Sustain us when we feel weary in the face of new challenges. Moderate our feelings when they become hostile towards others, and restrain us when we are inclined to hate those who bewilder or alarm us. And grant us the grace, O God, to seek a future in which justice and peace shall reign and where enemies are reconciled.

This psalm challenges us to reflect on whether our responses to irritation are proportionate and healthy, and if we feel that they are not to explore how we might modify them.

Psalm 144: Bow thy heavens

This, the last of the royal psalms, is envisaged as the prayer of the king. It begins and ends with the idea of 'blessing' – though commentators tell us that there are indeed different Hebrew words here; the first being a theological word of praise, so 'blessed' is appropriate, whereas at the end there is a word that refers to material fortune and this-worldly pleasure, so 'happy' works well. There is more than a hint of 'prosperity gospel' in these words, and certainly a strong sense of being a beneficiary of good fortune.

Verse 3 is an important clue. The wording is very like the opening of Psalm 8, but the meaning couldn't be more different. In Psalm 8 the thought is that human beings are wonderful, and while 'lower than the angels' humanity is nonetheless the crowning glory of the visible universe. The suggestion here, on the other hand, is that 'Man is like a thing of nought.' The progress from that very low spot to the happiness that comes at the end is not made by human effort. Indeed, the successes of life narrated in this psalm, which include strong sons and beautiful daughters, as well as full barns and thousands of sheep, not to mention powerful oxen and a lack of discontent on the street,[145] is a result of the people having 'the Lord for their God'. The way to this vision of worldly success is not easy, however, and it is clear from the opening that these rewards are not pure gift. Indeed, part of what the Lord has done is to have taught the poet to be a fighter. But the Lord's power is always important, especially when life gets difficult. Peterson's transliteration has a great phrase here, 'pull me out of the ocean of hate'.[146]

The writer of this psalm seems to be a negotiator as well as a fighter. The offer to sing a new song and play the lute is contingent on things working out well. Finally, there is such a strong sense of being surrounded by threat here that the reader might wonder whether the happiness announced at the end is actually yet achieved or still a matter of hope.

The prayer is for happiness.

Bless us, O Lord, with the gifts and qualities we need to achieve happiness in this life, protect us from the threat of war, terror and famine, and grant that we may have resource enough to make good homes and prosperous communities, and live to see our children flourish and our grandchildren thrive.

Aspects of this psalm may make us uncomfortable, but which is better, a prayer for what you think you should want or a prayer for what you truly want?

---

145 Alter translates this 'no screaming in our squares', p. 499.
146 Peterson, p. 192.

Psalm 145: The eyes of all

This psalm is viewed by some as the final psalm of substance in the Psalter and by others as a prelude or 'overture' to the doxological conclusion of the Book of Psalms. In fact, it can happily face both ways as it is a psalm of praise and yet it has more poetic substance, both in form and in content, than the five doxological psalms that follow. It is the final acrostic poem in the Psalter, and is recognized as 'an example of sophisticated poetic art'.[147]

The predominant dynamic is of the intensification of praise, with some powerful affirmations that recall the gracious, merciful and loving nature of the Lord. The structure, as might be expected with an acrostic, is that each verse punches out a new set of words and adds something unique to the whole. Not all the verses are equally memorable, but there are some that lodge in the mind, whether because of their natural poetry or because of their repeated use. As an example, one might cite the verse often used as a grace when the Latin translation is set to music,[148] 'The eyes of all wait upon thee, O Lord : and thou givest them their meat in due season.'

The psalm is confident in the kingship of the Lord, and ends with a vision of personal praise joining that of 'all flesh'.

The prayer is for patience.

Give us the patience, gracious God, that befits us and benefits others. Bless us with the ability to wait for our desires to be satisfied, the capacity to maintain calm when we are frustrated, the inclination to consider the needy when consumed by greed, and the tolerance that enables us to befriend those who disturb or disappoint us so that, biding your time, we may be fulfilled in due season.

The lovely image of eyes 'waiting' on God can be read as an invitation to deeper prayer – whether it is the contemplative prayer of loving attention or seen as the background to the petition for 'daily bread' in the Lord's Prayer.

---

147 Brueggemann and Bellinger, p. 603.
148 For instance, Charles Wood's 'Oculi Omnium'.

Psalm 146: While I live

The final five psalms all begin with the same word, 'Hallelujah', 'Praise the Lord!' They are all psalms of praise, and while there are intensely personal moments, their focus is on the qualities of God rather than the particular blessing that God has bestowed upon an individual, so 'praise' is the correct designation here, in contrast to 'thanksgiving'.

Psalm 146 turns on the tension that emerges between verses 3 and 5. We are inclined to trust 'princes' – but they are unreliable. It's not that they don't have power; it's that they won't have it for long. True power is praiseworthy and trustworthy and is only to be found in God, the creator.

It is after this is established that the justice-loving and kindly qualities of the Lord are enumerated and celebrated. In Psalm 144 we found more than a hint of a prosperity gospel, but in Psalm 146 we find the opposite, liberation theology, God's bias to the poor. The catalogue of those whom the Lord helps includes the oppressed and the hungry, those in prison and the blind, the 'fallen', bent or 'bowed down' and the righteous, and strangers, widows and orphans. But the Lord's interventions are not merely to support the weak. They also deal with those who act unjustly, 'as for the way of the ungodly, he turneth it upside down'. Ultimately, what is praiseworthy is the reliable, charitable, justice of the Lord.

The prayer is that we might trust wisely and act justly.

Guide us, gracious God, to be prudent and careful as we exercise trust, that we may not place our faith in those whose promises are vain, but work with those who seek to do your will and to see your kingdom come with freedom for the oppressed, food for the hungry, welcome for the stranger and justice for all who suffer at the hands of misguided human power.

The question of values might helpfully come to the fore as we come towards the end of the Psalter and enjoy its terminal crescendo of praise; in particular we might ask how our own sense of what is praiseworthy matches with that of the psalmists.

Psalm 147: The waters flow

This psalm is a celebration of faith and life and of God's loving actions. It is also a celebration of the joy of thanksgiving itself, 'yea, a joyful and pleasant thing it is to be thankful'. It covers a huge range of causes for gratitude. Beginning with thanks for the restoration of God's people and the rebuilding of Jerusalem after the return from exile in verses 1–6, it leads on to thanksgiving for the creation and sustaining of the natural world, taking especial pleasure in human beings for their human-ness in verses 7–11. This is followed by the manifest delight at being established as God's people in God's place.

The psalm ends with a poetic celebration in which the way the word of God is given is strangely but memorably compared with the coming of spring-like weather after a harsh burst of winter. 'He casteth forth his ice like morsels : who is able to abide his frost. / He sendeth out his word and melteth them : he bloweth with his wind, and the waters flow.'

In short, this is a psalm of confident celebration on a good day that comes from the lips of someone who remembers many bad days.

The prayer is about openness to God and the world.

As we sing your praise, O God, open our eyes to behold your wonder in the world, open our minds to appreciate the depth of your wisdom, and open our ears to hear your word; that our lives might flow in the ways that you have prepared for us, and that we may fulfil your will and enjoy all that is good and beautiful and true.

We often want to forget the detail of difficulties that we have lived through, but the challenge here is to let our thanksgiving cover the full range of our experiences.

Psalm 148: He spake the word

A psalm in two halves, Psalm 148 is an energetic and forceful invitation to praise God. The first half is addressed to the realms above, it is the 'the Lord of the heavens' who is to be praised. 'Praise him, all ye angels of his : praise him, all his host.' The 'heavens' here include the moon, stars and planets as well as the 'waters that are above the heavens'. These are all to praise God for their creation and their endless durability.

The second half is addressed to the inhabitants and elements of this world ranging from 'dragons and all deeps' through 'fire and hail, snow and vapours', 'mountains' 'worms and feathered fowls', 'kings and princes' and 'old men and children'. The reason for the praise is expressed only after much inviting, 'for his Name only is excellent, and his praise above heaven and earth'.

The final verse adds that there is renewed strength to be found in the God who is praised. This is another psalm that delights in both life and God and which breathes faith and confidence and joy.

The prayer expresses our desire to join with others in the praise of God.

Let us join our praise, O God, with all that has been made and with all that lives. Let us join our praise with all people who wonder at the magnificence and beauty of this world, and all who have faith in your love and seek to walk in your way.

The vision of unity in praise that this psalm creates has tremendous potential to inspire us to work for reconciliation in a fragmented world, and challenges us to ask ourselves what practical steps towards such reconciliation we might be able to take.

Psalm 149: Such honour

Psalm 149 is a short burst of praise that derives from a very specific context, a victory in battle. The first verses are an extended invitation to praise – including the line found in several other psalms, 'sing to the Lord a new song', which Alter wryly notes is 'a kind of self-advertisement of the psalmist, as if to say "here is a fresh and vibrant psalm that you have never heard before"'.[149] It is good to have this reminder of freshness and creativity as we get towards the very end of the collection. It is also a salutary reminder that at least some of the psalms that form part of the Christian scriptures are victory songs that derive from specific conflicts in the past which still have echoes in the conflicts of today and so may be heard very differently in different communities.

Verse 4 may read as if it is anticipating sentiments that come to full expression in Luke's song of Mary, but in this context the 'meek-hearted' whom 'the Lord helpeth' are not those of a modest or humble disposition, but those who were defeated in battle.[150]

The psalm ends with a number of bellicose and triumphalist sentiments such as, 'To bind their kings in chains : and their nobles with links of iron' which are perhaps understandable in the heat of the post-conflict moment, but are not particularly noble or gracious sentiments. It's not loving-kindness that is being celebrated here, but divine power that overcomes defeat and oppression.

The prayer is that our delight in the glory of God might have an impact both on our own lives and the wider world.

O God, to praise you is to sing a new song and to dance for joy; teach us to delight in your glory both when we are active and when we are at rest, and to let the love of your law inform the way we order our lives, our homes and our society, that joy might lead to justice, and that justice might inspire yet deeper joy.

We tend to get drawn into prayer for others when we are aware of their suffering, but might it not be just as valid to pray with those who are celebrating victory or liberation from oppression?

---

149 Alter, p. 512.
150 Alter translates this phrase, 'brought low by powerful enemies', p. 512.

Psalm 150: Every thing that hath breath

The final psalm in the book has the simplest possible structure. Envelope style, it begins and ends with 'Hallelujah', 'Praise the Lord.' Between is a series of ten imperatives, each a call to praise. Verses 1 and 2 focus on God's nature and acts, concluding with God's 'excellent greatness', and thereafter comes a wonderful catalogue of musical instruments with which God is to be praised. Within the list of various instruments to blow, pluck or strike there is also the invitation to dance the praise of God. The sense of energy, and perhaps even cacophony, builds across the few verses of this short psalm, each one getting slightly longer than the previous one, and coming to the peak of this crescendo with the double mention of cymbals, 'Praise him upon the well-tuned cymbals : praise him upon the loud cymbals.'

The final verse is an invitation to join in the same praise. The all-encompassing nature of this invitation is significant. It goes out not only to God's chosen people, nor even to all people, but to 'everything that has breath'; 'all that lives' is invited join in with this celebratory and enthusiastic praise of the Lord. This leads immediately to the very last word in the Psalter, 'Hallelujah' – Praise the Lord!

The prayer echoes the psalm's crescendo of praise.

O God, whose holiness surpasses our imagination and whose glory fills the skies, receive, we pray, our words and songs and hymns of praise. Thy acts are mighty! We praise thee. Thy greatness is excellent! We praise thee with voice and in song, in the whispers of our hearts, and in our mighty proclamations. We praise thee in word and in attitude, in demeanour and in action, and we implore all people who love life, everything that has breath, and all that exists, to share in our praise and to worship thee in thy great and unending glory.

Although there is genuine elation on having come to the end of the Psalter many of the issues touched on earlier will not yet be fully resolved. That is why the traditional approach to the psalms is to keep returning to the beginning and starting again.

Index of Themes

For others